GOOD DENTIST
POOR DENTIST

Proven Systems to Take Your
Practice from Average to Excellent

GOOD DENTIST
POOR DENTIST

Proven Systems to Take Your Practice from Average to Excellent

Kelli Strand Ngariki

Niche Pressworks
Indianapolis, IN

GOOD DENTIST, POOR DENTIST

Legal Disclaimer

The stories, names, characters, and incidents portrayed in this book are drawn from the author's experiences, knowledge, and imagination or have been adapted and modified to protect the privacy and confidentiality of individuals and organizations. Any resemblance to actual persons (living or deceased), businesses, or events is purely coincidental.

This book is intended solely for educational and informational purposes. It is not a substitute for professional legal, medical, or regulatory advice. The author and publisher assume no liability for any errors, omissions, or outcomes arising from the use of the information contained herein. Readers are advised to consult with qualified legal, compliance, or industry professionals for guidance on specific compliance or regulatory concerns.

The strategies and systems described in this book have contributed to the success of many dental practices. However, individual results will vary based on effort, consistency, and commitment to implementing the recommendations. Transformation requires dedication and persistence, much like providing quality patient care. While this book offers a roadmap, achieving success ultimately rests on your actions and determination.

For permission to reprint portions of this content or for bulk purchases, contact Support@GoodDentistBook.com.

Author Photograph by: Anne Nunn Photographers

Published by Niche Pressworks: NichePressworks.com
Indianapolis, IN

ISBN
eBook 978-1-962956-54-3
paperback 978-1-962956-55-0
hardback 978-1-962956-56-7

Library of Congress Cataloging-in-Publication Data on File at lccn.loc.gov

To my mom, dad, and husband — your unwavering support, love,
and belief in me have been my strength every step of the way.

And to my past and present employees — your hard work, passion,
and commitment have been the foundation of this business.
Each of you has brought unique talents, ideas, and perspectives
that have not only shaped the direction of our company
but also helped create a culture of excellence and care.

This book is a testament to all of you.
Thank you for inspiring me every day and
for being an essential part of this journey.

TABLE OF CONTENTS

YOUR PLAYBOOK
FOR SUCCESS

You don't have to see the whole staircase; just take the first step.
— MARTIN LUTHER KING JR.

Let's start with the truth: Compliance is not glamorous. In fact, I would guess it's not even something you ever thought about when deciding to become a dentist. This fact might be alarming to hear at the beginning of a book that seems to be about compliance.

Let me share a lesser-known and more important truth: Effective compliance is the backbone of every successful dental practice.

Setting up safety protocols and solid compliance strategies creates a safe dental practice. It also helps create systems that streamline operations, avoid penalties, and are the foundation of a smoothly run practice. When everyone knows what to do and when to do it, there's more time for patient care.

I started out as a middle school teacher, where I relied on organized systems to keep my classroom running smoothly. While that may seem like a very different career path, there are striking similarities. The systems I created for my classroom allowed me to enjoy the challenge of teaching and engaging with students. I ultimately decided to leave teaching after much reflection. I was at a school where the systems weren't supporting me or the students. The stress of inconsistent policies, lack of administrative support, and escalating challenges in the classroom left me dreading each day.

I was discussing these challenges over dinner with my aunt and uncle, Barb and Mark. They were in the process of finding a buyer for their compliance consulting business. Although they had asked me once before if I would be interested in buying the company, they chose this moment to gently ask if I'd reconsider their offer. At first, I hesitated, saying, "I don't know anything about compliance or dentists." But Mark changed my perspective by asking a simple question: "How did you manage your classroom?"

I explained how I set clear expectations and taught routines for every situation, from walking down the hall to turning in homework. Mark smiled and said, "That's all compliance is. Dentists are just better-behaved students. They need clear systems to follow so they can do things correctly."

Those words clicked. I realized my ability to create structures and teach processes was exactly what the business needed. By the end of the school year, I was a retired teacher and the proud owner of Healthcare Compliance Associates.

Since then, my business has helped hundreds of dentists build systems that simplify compliance, improve efficiency, and empower their teams. The same principles I used to teach students — clear expectations, structured routines, and accountability — have transformed dental practices into thriving, well-organized operations.

ALL SUCCESSFUL TEAMS HAVE SYSTEMS

Imagine a football team preparing to take the field for a big game. The energy is high, the fans are cheering, and the players are pumped. But as the whistle blows, there's chaos. The quarterback doesn't know what play to run, the receivers don't know which route to take, and the offense is scrambling. Every player is talented, but the team is doomed without a clear plan. Despite all their skill, if the players don't have a plan, they can't win.

Now, let's look at a winning team. The coaches create clear plans, then teach the team the exact plays and how to run them. Then, they practice — over and over again. Every player knows exactly where to be, what to do, and how to react in different situations. The quarterback knows the plays inside out and trusts his teammates to execute them flawlessly. When the game starts, it's almost effortless. The ball is snapped, the plays run smoothly, and the team moves like a finely tuned orchestra down the field to victory.

That's the power of having a game plan. In business, we call these plans systems or processes. Like in sports, a dental practice needs clear, repeatable processes. Each team member — from the front desk staff to the hygienists — should know their role and understand workflows so they can perform at their best. Without a system, it's like throwing your team onto the field without a playbook, expecting them to figure it out on the fly. But with a solid system, you create consistency and efficiency, and you trust that everything is handled correctly. This allows your team to win every time.

Systems refer to structured, repeatable processes designed to streamline operations, ensure compliance, and maintain consistency across a dental or business practice.

Think of systems as your playbook. They provide clear, step-by-step strategies to guide your team toward executing daily tasks with precision and consistency. Systems aren't just about processes; they're the game plan for success. They empower your team, ensure your patients' safety, and drive your practice to victory.

And here's the truth: Systems win championships.

Systems are your playbook for success!

WHY THIS BOOK?

Dentists must balance excellent patient care with the complexities of managing compliance, team dynamics, and operational efficiency. These demands can feel overwhelming, but they don't have to be. *Good Dentist, Poor Dentist* provides you with a practical, proven roadmap that will transform your practice into a thriving, compliant, and efficient operation.

The heart of this book is the SAFER Compliance System — a step-by-step framework designed specifically for dental practices to improve safety, streamline processes, and empower teams to perform at their best.

What makes this book different?

- **Process Guidance Tailored for Dental Practices**: Provides real-life examples and actionable steps customized for the unique needs of dental teams.
- **Proven Framework**: The SAFER Compliance System has helped many practices achieve compliance and operational success.
- **Supportive, Actionable Solutions**: Written by someone who understands the challenges dentists face, providing straightforward solutions to overcome them.

This book isn't just about compliance; it's about building a foundation for long-term success. By the end, you'll see compliance not as a burden but as an opportunity to strengthen your practice.

You will discover how small, actionable changes can transform your practice. But you don't have to do it alone. As you read, know that Healthcare Compliance Associates is here to guide you every step of the way. If you're ready to create safer, more efficient systems, visit **GoodDentistBook.com** to schedule a consultation and access resources tailored to your practice.

WHAT YOU'LL LEARN

Good Dentist, Poor Dentist will equip you to succeed. You'll learn how to:

- **Leverage the SAFER Compliance System**: Learn the five essential steps — Survey, Architect, Facilitate, Educate, and Review — that will transform your practice.
- **Enhance Team Performance**: Establish clear processes and empower your team with tools and training to excel in their roles.
- **Save Time and Money**: Minimize inefficiencies, reduce risks, and prevent costly mistakes with streamlined systems.
- **Prepare for Growth**: Create a scalable practice with the systems and structure to support future expansion or succession planning.

With these tools, you'll feel confident and prepared to take your practice to the next level. Let's start unlocking the full potential of your business through the power of systems.

Your Journey Starts Here

In the chapters ahead, you'll learn how to turn compliance into an asset rather than a headache. With our proven strategies, you can simplify your systems, boost efficiency, and enjoy the confidence of knowing your practice is fully protected and running smoothly. Building systems isn't about perfection; it's about progress. Every step brings you closer to the practice you wish you had.

Are you ready to create a safer, more efficient, and more profitable practice? With each chapter, you'll find that mastering these systems isn't just possible — it's incredibly rewarding. Ready to take that first step? Let's make it happen!

Not sure where to begin? Let me help you identify the most impactful systems for your team. Visit GoodDentistBook.com to book a consultation and start building your foundation today.

> *I feel more confident and comfortable knowing that*
> *I have compliance buttoned up and support when we need it.*
> *This has created a more positive environment at our workplace.*
> **— DR. BRIAN STANFORD**

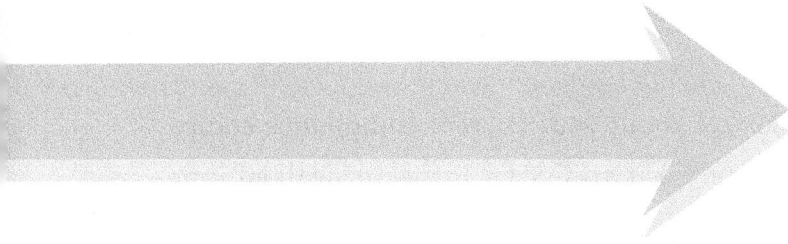

CHAPTER 1

COMPLIANCE: THE PROBLEM AND THE POSSIBILITY

By failing to prepare, you are preparing to fail.
— BENJAMIN FRANKLIN

Many dental practices run by default, following "the way it's always been done" and reacting to challenges as they arise. Does this sound familiar? While this approach may have worked in the past, it can't meet current safety and operational demands. Luckily, implementing compliance systems can help practices shift from a reactive response to proactive management.

In this way, compliance creates a set of systems and clear processes that give employees confidence, provide patients with a reliable experience, and make your practice more organized and ready to grow. It's time to stop thinking of your office as a collection of people, products, and equipment. Instead, start seeing it as a set of systems that can consistently deliver high-quality dental care efficiently and safely — every time.

Let's begin by assessing how you feel about your current compliance setup. Consider this question: What would you do if an OSHA inspector walked into your practice tomorrow? Would you feel prepared, or would you panic? Let's look at how one dentist felt in just such a situation.

THE $20,000 WAKE-UP CALL

The morning started like any other at Dr. Tim Baker's dental practice. Hygienists reviewed charts, assistants set up trays, and Sally, the office manager, reviewed the schedule at the front desk. Then the front door opened.

A tall man walked in, wearing jeans and a button-down shirt and holding a black carrier bag. His lanyard, marked with a white name tag and photo, caught Sally's attention. "Good morning," she said with a smile, "How can I help you?"

"I'm Dave Picket with Oregon OSHA. I'm here to inspect your facility."

Sally's smile froze. "Just a minute," she stammered and rushed off to find Dr. Baker.

As she passed hygienists and assistants, she whispered, "OSHA's here! OSHA's here!"

Standing in the doctor's doorway, she blurted, "OSHA's here. What do we do?"

Dr. Baker's eyes widened as he looked up from his computer screen. "Oh sh*&, I don't know," he said, hurrying with her to the reception area to meet the inspector.

Caught off guard, his team nearly stumbled over one another. They had never discussed or planned for an OSHA inspection and didn't know what to expect or, more importantly, what to do.

After a quick handshake, Dave began, "This is a routine inspection. I'll start by reviewing your documentation."

Trying to appear composed, Dr. Baker asked, "Which documentation, specifically?"

"Let's start with your bloodborne pathogen plan, hazard communications plan, and safety plan," Dave replied.

Dr. Baker nodded, "Sure, just give me a minute."

He quickly motioned to Sally, who followed him back to his office. Once out of earshot, he whispered, "He wants to see our plans for blood and hazards. Do we have anything like that?"

Sally thought for a moment, then nodded, "Oh, right! We bought that ADA binder. I bet the plans are in there."

After finally locating the binder, Dr. Baker returned to reception and handed it to Dave before realizing it was still in the plastic shrink wrap. The inspector looked down at the unopened binder and said, "How can these be your plans when you haven't even opened them?"

Things went downhill from there. Dave moved through the inspection, pointing out hazards in the instruments processing area and asking Dr. Baker about their PPE Hazard Assessment and policies on PPE use. Dr. Baker had no answers, and the staff's responses varied, with each person seemingly operating on their own informal system.

"I've identified several hazards that haven't been sufficiently addressed. You don't have a plan of action, and your employees don't seem clear on your safety expectations." Dave continued, "You'll get my report in a few weeks, and I'll follow up to make sure you're making progress on these issues. I expect that when I come back, the wrapper will be off the book, and you and your staff will have clear plans in place."

A week and a half later, Dr. Baker received Dave's full report, outlining all the citations and fines totaling nearly $20,000. The report also included the corrective action plan Dr. Baker was required to follow and report on to ensure compliance within a set timeframe. **This was a painful wake-up call. More than the money, it was the realization that his team and his patients deserved better.**

Shaken and humbled, Dr. Baker called his team together. He asked, "How are we supposed to know all this stuff?"

Keri, his lead dental assistant, said, "When I worked at Dr. Bannon's office, a company came in every year to do our training and got us all set up. They were very helpful."

Dr. Baker didn't hesitate, "Okay, see how soon they can come out."

That's when Keri contacted Healthcare Compliance Associates. We scheduled a visit for the following week, bringing along an easy-to-use OSHA manual complete with plans and policies. We trained the entire staff on the essential requirements. We provided extra one-on-one support to Keri, the newly appointed safety officer, to ensure she felt confident in her new role. Then, we helped them create documented systems for critical tasks like spore testing and eyewash flushing.

When Dave returned two months later for the follow-up inspection, he stated, "I'm very impressed with your progress. You've been able to correct or minimize the hazards on my initial report."

Dr. Baker and his team exchanged high-fives, their relief and sense of accomplishment apparent in their smiles. For the first time, Dr. Baker felt confident that his practice was meeting OSHA standards and functioning at a level he didn't even realize was possible. His team was stronger, more aligned, and better equipped to handle challenges, and Dr. Baker couldn't help but feel grateful for the transformation they had achieved together.

> *For the first time, Dr. Baker felt confident that his practice was meeting OSHA standards and functioning at a level he didn't even realize was possible.*

Building a Playbook for Success

Dr. Baker's experience is not unique. Many practices rely on informal knowledge and verbal instructions to get through the day. But when challenges arise, whether it's an OSHA inspection, staff turnover, or a patient complaint, these gaps in preparation become glaring liabilities.

Here's the truth: A successful practice isn't built on improvisation. It's designed and cultivated through systems.

Systems, or standardized processes, are your playbook for success. They ensure that every team member knows their role, tasks are performed consistently, and compliance becomes second nature — not a last-minute scramble. For Dr. Baker, implementing systems transformed his practice from reactive chaos to confident efficiency.

Dr. Baker's experience mirrors what we've seen countless times — dental practices operating in reactive mode, hoping that problems won't surface. But hope isn't a strategy.

Prepare for an OSHA Inspection

- Organize critical compliance documents, such as bloodborne pathogens, hazard communications, and emergency action plans.
- Create a safety binder to organize all your plans and policies.
- Draft a simple guide for what to do if an inspector arrives unannounced.
- Role-play possible OSHA Inspector questions with the team — e.g., Where is your spill kit? Where are your safety records and documentation? Where are your fire extinguishers?
- Check the OSHA website for your state (and federal) rules and review the inspection guidelines.

THE POWER OF SYSTEMS

Standardizing systems eliminates disorganization and brings clarity to your practice. I discovered the power of systems firsthand after taking ownership of Healthcare Compliance Associates. During the first week, I was nervous and excited to get started. That week passed in a blur, filled with learning and putting out fires as they came up. But by Friday morning, I had a growing sense of dread and thought, "Oh my gosh, what have I done? Am I in over my head?"

I knew I needed help. Luckily, I had heard about a free mentorship program called SCORE. I contacted them, and a mentor named Frank arrived at my door the following week.

His pleasant voice exuded an air of quiet confidence. He asked me to tell him a little bit about my business. After giving him a quick overview, he told me in a very matter-of-fact tone, "You need to run your business like a franchise."

With a sideways look, I responded, "I just bought this company; I cannot imagine franchising."

He explained, "You don't have to franchise the company; you just need to run your business like one. Successful franchises rely on four basic systems that work together. By focusing on these, you'll take control of your business." Frank explained each system, and I didn't realize yet the impact this would have on my business:

1. **Document Systems**

   Every task needs a step-by-step guide. Create clear procedures for every aspect of the business. These systems act as a blueprint, ensuring tasks are performed consistently, regardless of who is doing them. In a dental practice, for instance, some important systems to document include protocols for patient intake, instrument sterilization procedures, and room turnover processes. By standardizing how things are done, teams know what to expect, which means they can work together more efficiently and deliver a better patient experience.

2. **Standardize Daily Operations**

   Using the documented procedures, it's then possible to standardize daily activities, ensuring that every team member completes tasks in the same way to maintain consistency across the board. For example, a standardized operatory turnover process ensures that rooms are cleaned, disinfected, and prepared for the next patient in the exact same way every time. This ensures safety and avoids errors. It also improves work quality and makes it easier to train and onboard new employees.

3. **Organize Training Programs**

   Training programs give employees the tools they need to succeed and are the cornerstone of a successful business. Investing in comprehensive, role-specific training ensures that every team member has the knowledge and skills to excel. For dental practices, training programs include effective onboarding for new hires, required compliance training (like OSHA, HIPAA, and infection control), and teaching the documented systems. Additionally, providing continuous education opportunities for the team improves employee satisfaction and promotes retention.

4. **Log and Audit Systems**

   To guarantee excellence, each of these three systems needs to be monitored and maintained. Without reviewing your systems, you have no idea whether your team is doing what you expect of them. For this reason, it's essential to use logs and regular audits to monitor and maintain high standards. Logs for tracking waterline testing, equipment maintenance, and sterilization processes provide accountability, create a record of compliance, and can play a huge role in preventing fines if OSHA shows up at your practice. Audits allow clinics to evaluate their systems' effectiveness, identify improvement areas, and ensure protocols are followed. For instance, periodic audits of patient charting or infection control measures can catch discrepancies early, preventing more significant issues down the road.

Together, these four principles gave me a way to approach my new business, and ultimately, I adapted these to meet the unique needs of dental compliance. As Frank put it, "Think of these as the pillars of a successful business, whether you want to stay the same size or expand." This led me to develop the SAFER Compliance Systems framework.

> *Think of these as the pillars of a successful business,*
> *whether you want to stay the same size or expand.*

Many years later, I realized just how right he was. Everything boils down to those four things. My business still runs seamlessly, even in my absence. These principles are just as powerful in dental practices. Imagine having clear protocols for patient intake, sterilization, and operatory turnover. With structured systems, your team will know exactly what to do — every time.

HOW SYSTEMS COULD SAVE YOU $20,000

Dr. Baker's $20,000 mistake wasn't due to malice or incompetence; it was caused by a lack of preparation. Like many dental practice owners, he assumed compliance could wait. That assumption backfired when an OSHA inspector arrived unannounced, catching Dr. Baker and his team off guard.

Without a clear compliance plan, they scrambled to locate materials and guessed at answers to critical safety questions. The result? $20,000 in fines, a corrective action plan, and weeks of unnecessary stress.

Mistakes like these are preventable. With clear systems in place, Dr. Baker's team could have confidently faced the inspection, avoided the fines, and focused on what matters most — delivering exceptional patient care. Here's how systems can safeguard your practice:

- **Consistency.** Systems ensure every team member knows their role, delivering the same high-quality care to every patient. For example, a standardized operatory turnover process guarantees that rooms are cleaned and disinfected thoroughly every time, reducing risks and improving patient care and satisfaction.

- **Efficiency.** With a well-documented game plan, your team spends less time scrambling and more time providing excellent care. Imagine eliminating uncertainty during busy periods — your systems are the playbook that keeps everything running smoothly.

- **Safety and Compliance.** Systems integrate essential regulations, making compliance part of your daily routine. For instance, a documented sterilization protocol ensures OSHA and CDC standards are met while creating peace of mind for your team.

- **Scalability.** Expanding your practice? Systems provide the foundation for growth. They simplify onboarding for new hires and ensure your growing team can maintain the same high-quality standards without feeling overwhelmed.

THE PERFECT PAIR: SYSTEMS AND COMPLIANCE

When I became a business owner, I was determined to provide the best possible service to my clients. I worked to become an expert on compliance, immersing myself in OSHA, HIPAA, and infection prevention regulations. I thought that understanding compliance would be enough. But I quickly realized something critical: Compliance without systems is dangerous — it can lead to inconsistencies, mistakes, and vulnerabilities that can put your team, patients, and practice at risk.

Clear, documented systems turn compliance from a source of stress into a tool for peace of mind. They provide your team with structure and eliminate uncertainty from daily operations. For instance, having a step-by-step protocol for PPE use ensures safety and empowers your team to do their jobs confidently, knowing exactly what PPE to wear during each activity.

Many of our clients come to us when they're stuck. They're frustrated that employees aren't following proper protocols and don't know what to do. After telling us a bit about their challenges and desired outcomes, it becomes clear that many of these offices rely on unwritten rules and verbal guidance, which leaves too much room for misinterpretation. Our advice is always simple: "You need a written plan. Follow up regularly to ensure employees are adhering to the plan and hold them accountable, using the policy as your reference."

This straightforward solution is often underestimated — yet it can have a significant impact. By pairing compliance with clear, streamlined systems, we help practices lay the foundation for consistency, safety, and efficiency. To help clients manage the shift toward systematized operations, we started developing detailed standard operating procedures (SOPs), turning compliance guidelines into actionable, step-by-step templates. From start-of-day protocols to waterline testing, these customizable SOPs form the core of the SAFER Compliance Systems approach — a powerful combination of compliance and efficiency that's transforming dental practices.

> Standard operating procedures (SOPs) turn compliance guidelines into actionable, step-by-step templates.

The best part? You don't have to reinvent the wheel. With the right tools and support, you can implement these systems quickly and effectively, transforming compliance from a burden into an advantage. In the coming pages, you'll see how our SAFER Compliance Systems approach can be used to implement systems that will ensure your practice thrives with greater efficiency and less stress.

> The value of a system is how it saves time, reduces errors, and increases profitability.
> **— PAUL AKERS**

TAKE ACTION: CONDUCT A SIMPLE SELF-ASSESSMENT

The path forward starts with a simple self-assessment. Take a few moments now to reflect on what's happening at your practice. Write your responses below.

1. **Identify where you feel the most stress.** Look for common pain points: compliance gaps, workflow inefficiencies, or team frustration.

   _____

   _____

   _____

   _____

   _____

2. **Imagine what success looks like.** A streamlined, thriving practice isn't just a dream. Picture how small, steady changes could transform your team, patient experience, and daily operations.

   _____

   _____

   _____

   _____

   _____

3. **Take the first step.** Even small wins like documenting a protocol or optimizing one task build momentum. List one process you want to streamline.

   _____

   _____

   _____

   _____

   _____

CHAPTER 2

THE PRACTICE YOU'VE ALWAYS WANTED

*The difference between where you are and
where you want to be lies in your willingness to
embrace change and the systems that make it possible.*
— UNKNOWN

Have you ever felt there is unnecessary stress in your practice for you or your staff? What steps have you taken to address this? If quick-fix compliance programs or ineffective online training have left you frustrated, don't worry — this process is different. We've developed and refined this proven method after years of working with clients and by applying it successfully in our own business.

WHY IT'S WORTH THE EFFORT

Many dental professionals resist change because it seems overwhelming or time-consuming. But the real risk isn't in starting — it's in doing nothing. The consequences of inaction can include employee turnover, complaints to OSHA, accidents or injuries, fines, lawsuits, and damage to your reputation.

> *I knew I needed systems, but the project felt so overwhelming that I kept putting it off. Small mistakes started slipping through, and we were scrambling to fix them after the fact. Now, with written systems in place, I feel confident knowing my team is supported, my business is protected, and my workplace is thriving.*
> — DR. BRIAN STANFORD, TRANSFORM DENTISTRY

This process isn't complicated. Small, actionable steps lead to significant results that impact your team, business, and bottom line. Imagine your practice running like a well-oiled machine, with fewer frantic moments and more time to focus on growth and innovation.

What would stress-free operations and consistent excellence mean for you? Beyond avoiding fines and safety incidents, systems give you peace of mind, knowing everything is handled correctly. If you're ready to move from hoping your practice is safe to knowing it is, keep reading to discover how to transform your compliance programs — and your life.

WHERE ARE YOU NOW?

Systematizing your business represents a fundamental change. Many people view compliance as just another government hoop they must jump through. To fully benefit from this book, I encourage you to set aside these ideas and open your mind to the possibility that compliance systems can actually take your business to the next level.

As described in David Jenyns' book *SYSTEMology*,[1] businesses typically progress through four stages: Survival, Steady, Growth, and Exit. Knowing where you stand is key to deciding your next steps.

Survival Stage. Often, new practices operate on memory rather than systems, leaving them vulnerable to inefficiencies and constant "firefighting." For example, they scramble to meet OSHA requirements during an inspection instead of maintaining year-round compliance.

Steady Stage. Practices with undocumented processes often depend on one organized team member, such as an office manager, to keep things running. While effective in the short term, high turnover or staff absences can disrupt operations.

Growth Stage. With systems linked to policies, scaling becomes possible. Routine tasks can be delegated, freeing up skilled employees for higher-value work. For instance, hiring a sterile tech to streamline instrument processing allows dental assistants to focus on patient care, improving satisfaction and efficiency.

Exit Stage. A practice with robust systems becomes a turnkey operation that is attractive to buyers and resilient to change. Even if selling isn't your goal, this level of systematizing allows you to step away without worrying about disruptions.

---

1   David Jenyns, *SYSTEMology: Create Time, Reduce Errors and Scale Your Profits with Proven Business Systems* (Austin, TX: SYSTEMology, 2020).

BUSINESS STAGES

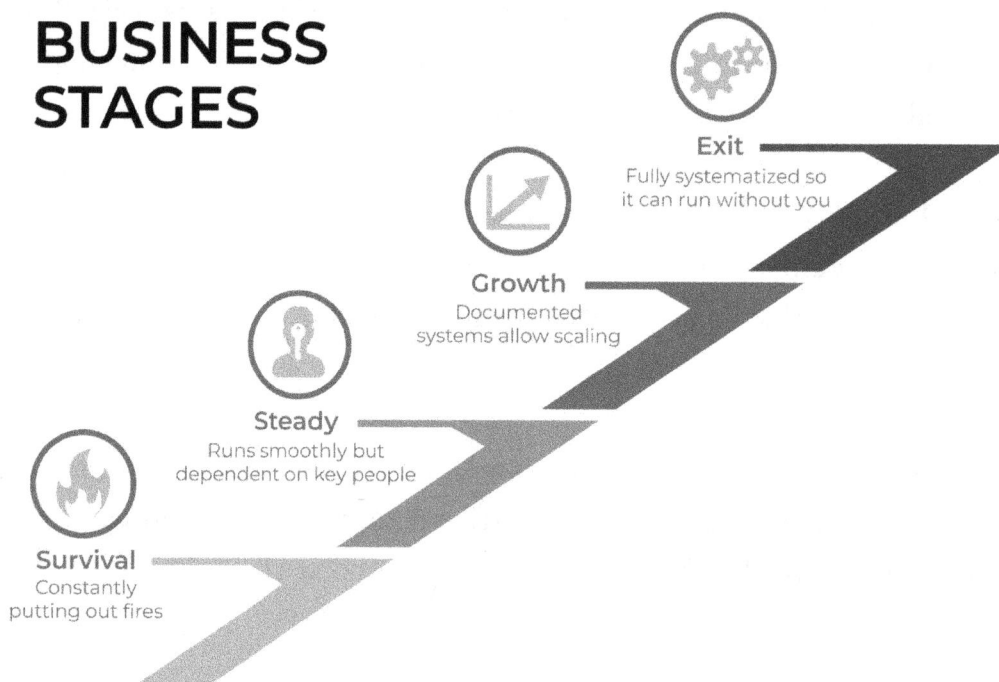

Exit
Fully systematized so
it can run without you

Growth
Documented
systems allow scaling

Steady
Runs smoothly but
dependent on key people

Survival
Constantly
putting out fires

Figure 1. Business stages based on David Jenyns' four stages of growth.

Are You Where You Want to Be?

Think about your current stage. Are you satisfied, or do inefficiencies, frustrations, or burnout weigh you down? Are the hours you put in bringing you closer to your goals, or are they draining your energy and costing you time and anxiety?

Systematization isn't just about growth; it's about reclaiming control, reducing stress, and aligning your practice with your vision. Whether your goal is to scale, spend more time with loved ones, or simply take a well-deserved break, building systems can transform both your business and your personal life.

THE POWER OF PROTOCOLS: A PRACTICE TRANSFORMED

Let's look at an example of a practice where the dentist decided they weren't where they wanted to be, and they contacted us. Before working with Healthcare Compliance Associates (HCA), Riverstone Dentistry faced significant challenges in managing compliance. The lead dentist, Dr. Tanya, described a hectic environment with high turnover and varying employee experience levels. These factors led to inconsistent practices.

"We had employees coming in with their own ways of doing things — some with no dental or infection control experience at all," she explained. This lack of uniformity resulted in trust issues among team members, particularly in critical areas like room sterilization and setup. It strained relationships and left Dr. Tanya uncertain whether compliance standards were being met.

The tipping point came when she realized that high turnover rates and a shrinking pool of skilled, motivated workers were the new reality. As the practice grew busier, relying on one-on-one training became increasingly difficult — too time-consuming, inconsistent, and inefficient, especially for employees with little to no experience.

"We tried reminding employees how things should be done, but without written protocols, accountability was nearly impossible," Dr. Tanya admitted. She realized that relying on verbal instructions or memory wasn't sustainable. In order to keep growing the business, something had to change. Specifically, the practice needed a structured system that employees could refer to consistently.

Riverstone Dentistry's relationship with HCA began with some uncertainty. Having worked with HCA's previous owners, the team wasn't sure what to expect under new leadership. However, they were also optimistic about the possibility of fresh ideas to energize their office.

What surprised them most was how thorough and detail-oriented our process was. Our customized evaluations and hands-on recommendations were tailored to their specific needs and provided immediate value. Dr. Tanya even noted, "HCA helped us identify our problems and then provided practical solutions. Their written protocols and follow-ups were exactly what we needed."

During COVID, the practice experienced an additional benefit. During this stressful and unpredictable time, we continually provided clients with proactive updates and guidance. Dr. Tanya recalls being amazed at how HCA was able to stay on top of the situation, helping their team navigate uncertainty with clarity and confidence.

The transition wasn't without its challenges. Employees initially felt unsure but were open to the changes. Their willingness to engage with the new systems and HCA's detailed protocols helped the team align their efforts and expectations.

"Change of any kind takes time to adapt to," Dr. Tanya shared, "And I'm pleased with how the team took on the new challenges and committed to the process."

With multiple employees working on different days, getting everyone up to speed required additional coordination. However, everyone gradually embraced the new system, motivated by a shared commitment to improving patient and employee safety.

The turning point came when Dr. Tanya noticed the back office flowing smoothly for the first time in years. Team members operated with confidence, knowing exactly what was expected of them. Questions dwindled, and employees relied on the written protocols when needed.

"The team seemed happier and more confident, and there was far less frustration. Seeing operations performed consistently and correctly made all the difference," Dr. Tanya recalled.

Since partnering with HCA, Riverstone Dentistry has seen significant improvements in its compliance program and team dynamics. With up-to-date protocols, checklists, and written procedures in place, the practice now operates with far greater efficiency and confidence.

"The biggest relief is knowing we have current protocols and tools to support our team," she said.

Dr. Tanya's advice to other dental practices facing similar challenges is clear: "Have all protocols in writing and ensure everyone understands that THIS is how we do it. Trust the professionals at HCA — they are thorough, organized, and genuinely want to help. Trust the process, and you'll find yourself with a happier, more efficient team."

> *Have all protocols in writing and ensure everyone understands that THIS is how we do it. Trust the professionals at HCA — they are thorough, organized, and genuinely want to help. Trust the process, and you'll find yourself with a happier, more efficient team.*

Riverstone Dentistry's transformation highlights the power of clear systems and compliance. By implementing structured protocols and tools, the practice turned inconsistency into certainty, improving team morale, patient care, and daily operations. Employees felt empowered and supported, fostering trust and accountability.

Dr. Tanya's journey shows that while change can be challenging, it's worth the effort. Let Riverstone Dentistry's experience inspire you to take the steps needed to build a better future for your team and patients.

Choosing the Right Compliance Consulting Firm

Look for a compliance consulting firm that offers these key services:

1. **OSHA Training for Your State:** Stay current with dental-specific regulations.
2. **Flexible Onsite and Online Training:** Perfect for busy dental teams.
3. **Onboarding Help:** Simplify compliance for new hires.
4. **Regular Updates:** Stay ahead with alerts on rule changes.
5. **Onsite Evaluations:** Identify gaps and get tailored guidance.
6. **Custom Documentation:** Hard copy or digital forms to fit your needs.

WHAT'S THE COST OF NOT DOING IT?

Who is ultimately responsible for the safety of your patients and employees? You! Imagine the consequences of a significant failure at your practice. Lacking formal systems not only creates inefficiencies but also introduces significant risks.

For instance, one practice we worked with did not know they needed to conduct regular waterline testing. As a result, they didn't realize their dental unit waterlines had become contaminated. It wasn't until a patient developed an infection that they traced the problem back to insufficient testing protocols. The oversight resulted in costly treatments for the patient, shaken trust, and a mandatory inspection of their infection control practices.

This incident underscores the importance of having proactive systems in place. Simple, well-documented protocols — like quarterly waterline testing — could have prevented the issue entirely.

Think about the trust patients place in you every day. The costs of noncompliance aren't just financial; they can involve the well-being of your patients, irreparable damage to your reputation, and even the future of your practice.

One client noted, "Before implementing proper systems, we were constantly worried about compliance issues, which distracted us from patient care."

Noncompliance with OSHA and HIPAA regulations and infection control guidelines can have significant financial and operational repercussions for dental practices. Here are some eye-opening facts that reveal some of the very real risks:

- **OSHA Violations**
  - One dental practice was fined $53,000 for common OSHA violations, underscoring the substantial penalties that can arise from noncompliance.
  - The penalty for a serious violation of OSHA standards ranges from $1,200 to $16,000, emphasizing the financial risks associated with noncompliance.

- **HIPAA Violations**
  - In 2024, over 150 HIPAA cases resulted in civil money penalties of over $145 million, that's nearly $1 million per case.
  - In 2024, HIPAA violations ranged from $1,000 to an annual cap of $1.5 million.[2]

- **Dental Infection Control Breaches**
  - In severe cases, failure to adhere to infection control protocols can result in the loss of a dental license. A notable example is Dr. William Do, DDS, who had his license revoked by the Dental Board of California after failing to comply with infection control standards and neglecting to address identified issues.[3]
  - Small infection control breaches occur daily in most dental clinics. These breaches can lead to both minor and major health issues.

---

2 U.S. Department of Health and Human Services, Office for Civil Rights, "HIPAA Enforcement Highlights," last modified October 31, 2024, https://www.hhs.gov/hipaa/for-professionals/compliance-enforcement/data/enforcement-highlights/index.html.

3 Cameron Cortigiano, "California Dentist's License Revoked Over Infection Control Violations," *Becker's Dental Review,* May 2, 2024, accessed February 3, 2025, https://www.beckersdental.com/dentists/43589-california-dentists-license-revoked-over-infection-control-violations.html.

Common problems include inadequate hand hygiene, failing to wear safety glasses (often only wearing regular prescription glasses), and not removing gowns before leaving the treatment area.

These statistics illustrate that neglecting compliance can lead to substantial financial penalties, legal liabilities, and damage to a practice's reputation. Implementing robust compliance programs can help mitigate these risks and ensure the safety and privacy of both patients and staff.

SET YOUR BUSINESS UP FOR SUCCESS

Hopefully, by now, you are looking at your business in a new way — not as a collection of individuals, equipment, and jobs but rather as a series of interconnected systems. When these systems are documented and consistently followed, they can transform your practice into a "lean, mean money-making machine." That doesn't mean your only motivation should be profit; in fact, you will likely also develop systems that focus on how employees treat and interact with patients. So, perhaps I should say a "lean, kind money-making machine." Michael Gerber, in *E-Myth Revisited,* says it another way: "Systems run the business, and people run the systems."

Remember, compliance ensures your practice adheres to laws, regulations, and standards. Compliance systems provide structured, repeatable processes that consistently follow these regulations throughout the practice. By systematizing compliance, you create a framework where every employee knows exactly how to execute essential safety tasks. These systems reduce the risk of fines and legal issues, streamline operations, and improve overall efficiency.

Integrating compliance into your business systems ensures that tasks like patient care, sterilization, and safety protocols are followed correctly, every time, without relying on memory or guesswork. This consistency leads to better patient outcomes, a safer workplace, and reduced risks.

THE CHOICE IS CLEAR

You've seen all the options, and you have three choices:

1. **Keep doing what you've been doing.**
    With this choice, you just keep doing what you've been doing. Ignore any opportunities to improve your business, and don't access the power of compliance protocols. You'll likely continue to struggle with employee turnover, feeling like there's never enough time, and a continuing drain of your emotional energy and financial resources. You'll also live with the constant fear of an infection control breach or OSHA inspection — and the devastating consequences they bring.

2. **Do compliance yourself.**
    Organizing compliance in-house takes commitment, time, and exceptional attention to detail. Here's a short list of what needs to be addressed:

    ○ Research OSHA, HIPAA, and infection control regulations (Note: Some are state-specific).

    ○ Conduct a thorough hazard assessment of your facility.

    ○ Write detailed plans and policies for your team, ensuring they're reviewed annually.

    ○ Develop a training program for new employees and schedule yearly training for the entire team.

    ○ Stay updated with changing regulations and make adjustments as needed.

Managing this in-house is certainly possible — many clinics have tried it. But before diving in, ask yourself: **Is this the best use of my time and energy?**

Let me share a parallel. We pay a skilled IT professional to manage our cybersecurity and tech issues because that's their expertise — not ours. If we tried to do it ourselves, we'd waste hours troubleshooting small problems, likely miss critical details, and still end up with subpar results. It's the same reason we wouldn't build our own website — it would take us three times as long, look amateurish, and ultimately drain us of time and energy that could be better spent elsewhere.

Compliance is no different. You could spend countless hours researching government websites, trying to interpret legal jargon, developing documentation, and delivering training. But here's the truth:

- It will take significantly more time than you think.
- You won't have anyone to call when you hit roadblocks or have questions.
- The result will likely lack the polish and thoroughness of a professional's work.

Even if you "figure it out," this DIY approach can lead to gaps in compliance, exposing your practice to risk — and the time lost is time you could have spent on patient care or practice growth.

3. **Call in the experts and relax!**
   By bringing in a team of compliance professionals to handle the complexities of OSHA, HIPAA, and infection control regulations, you delegate the task to experts. They'll do the following:

   - Ensure your practice stays compliant with current guidelines.
   - Supply all necessary documentation.
   - Deliver tailored training for your team.
   - Help you create clear, documented systems for everyone to follow.

With experts managing the details, you can focus on what truly matters. Imagine the relief of knowing every compliance detail is covered, freeing up your time and energy to focus on what you love most about your work. Your team will thank you, and your practice will thrive.

> *Do not try to approach the task on your own.*
> *Find a group of professionals you trust to help give you guidance*
> *and direction. This makes life so much easier and less stressful.*
> **— DR. BRIAN, TRANSFORM DENTAL**

Compliance and systematization are the foundation of an efficient, successful practice. By embracing proven systems, you protect your practice from costly mistakes, empower your team, and deliver exceptional patient care.

The choice is clear: Continue with the status quo and risk burnout and inefficiencies OR invest in systems and professional support to elevate your practice to new heights.

Taking the first step will transform your business and give you the freedom to focus on what matters most. The choice is yours — but the best path is obvious.

Start Building the Practice You Deserve

Stop reacting to problems and start designing the practice you've always wanted. The SAFER Compliance System will help you simplify, systematize, and succeed. It's not about working harder — it's about working smarter.

Let's get started. The future of your practice begins today.

> *A good system shortens the road to the goal.*
> **— ORISON SWETT MARDEN**

Improving your practice doesn't mean starting from scratch. Begin by recognizing the systems that already work well in your office and use those successes as a foundation for solving new challenges.

Celebrate What's Working

Take a moment to consider and write down the processes in your practice that consistently run smoothly. These systems are already contributing to your success. Examples might include:

- *An effective patient reminder system*
- *A reliable operatory turnover process*
- *A streamlined morning huddle that keeps everyone on the same page*

Example: "Our patient intake process is so organized! It sets a great tone for the day."

Acknowledging these wins will build confidence and help you see the value of systematizing other areas.

_____

_____

_____

_____

_____

_____

_____

_____

_____

_____

CHAPTER 3

SHIFTING PERSPECTIVE DRIVES CHANGE

Your only limit is the belief that you have one.
— UNKNOWN

By now, you're starting to see how systems can transform your practice. But you may encounter resistance to change. Many dental teams oppose new systems because of commonly held myths and fears: "Systems are only for big practices," "It will take too much time," or "Employees won't like rigid rules." But honestly, this kind of thinking is what holds practices back, leading to inefficiencies, stress, and burnout.

The truth? Effective systems empower success. They organize tasks in a logical manner that optimizes each employee's time, turning frustration into confidence and uncertainty into clarity.

By challenging myths and fears, you can create a practice that's safer, more efficient, and far less stressful. Linda's story illustrates what happens when myths and limiting beliefs prevent a practice from implementing systems. Her situation was a perfect storm of fear and inaction: an inexperienced doctor, a domineering office manager, and a lack of systems to protect the team. The result? Frustration, fear, and a practice operating in disarray.

LINDA'S STORY: A TURNING POINT

I headed into a ground-floor room with beige wall panels, a little wooden podium, and rows of dark gray conference chairs. I was the guest speaker at the Oregon Dental Conference in Portland, Oregon, and about sixty dental professionals filled the room.

Throughout the presentation, I asked for and encouraged questions and audience participation. Linda, a participant in the third row, asked many rhetorical questions, like, "So, we're supposed to be flushing our eyewash station weekly and documenting it, right?"

Toward the end of the presentation, I discussed personal protective equipment (PPE) and the requirements for when to wear it. Linda asked, "What if the office manager only allows us a certain number of gloves each day?"

"It's the employer's responsibility to provide appropriate PPE to every employee with potential exposure," I said.

"Yes, but what if they don't?" she said, barely holding back her frustration. She clutched the OSHA manual in her hands.

I asked, "Have you talked to the doctor about it? He's the one responsible, not the office manager."

She replied, "He's a new, young doctor, and he does whatever the office manager tells him to do. We also have new assistants who don't clean and sterilize instruments correctly, but when I tell them, they don't do anything, and no one backs me up."

I walked toward her and said, "Your dentist is liable for all of this, and he's putting his license on the line by not complying."

At that, a woman in the back of the room blurted, "If you are a dental hygienist, your license is also on the line!"

Linda's eyes widened, "I hadn't thought of that," she admitted.

The woman from the back spoke up again. "You need to protect yourself and your patients. If your doctor doesn't listen, we've got an opening at our office."

Reassuring Linda, I added, "Talk to him about it as an opportunity rather than a criticism. Remind him that safety is important for patients, for keeping employees happy, and for minimizing his liability."

The encouragement seemed to bring a flicker of hope to Linda's eyes. "Thank you," she said. "I needed to hear that."

After the presentation ended, Linda approached me and said, "I'm going to talk to him. I can't keep doing this without support."

As she left, I knew that, regardless of her doctor's response, Linda had made a choice. She wasn't going to sit back anymore. She was going to advocate for herself, her team, and her patients.

I later learned that the following Monday, she discussed her safety concerns with the doctor. "Do you realize that Christina only gives us a certain number of gloves every day, and she won't give us more?"

The doctor looked puzzled, "What? Why would she do that?"

"I assume to save money," she answered.

He moved out from behind his desk and said, "Let me go talk to Christina. I'm sure this is just a misunderstanding."

Linda could feel her face getting hot as she watched him walk out the door.

After several minutes, the doctor returned with Christina. Christina had a smile on her face, which confused Linda. The doctor said, "It turns out this was just a big misunderstanding. Christina explained that we were just low on gloves that week."

Christina put her hand on Linda's shoulder and said, "Honey, you can use as many as you need."

Linda managed a small smile and said, "Okay," as she walked out of the room.

That evening, Linda replayed the meeting in her mind. She couldn't shake the feeling that her concerns had been dismissed. The dentist's explanation of a "misunderstanding" felt like a way to avoid accountability, and Christina's patronizing smile only deepened her frustration.

For months, Linda had tried to advocate for better practices, bringing her concerns to the office manager, her colleagues, and the dentist. But it had become clear: Her voice wasn't being heard, and patient safety wasn't a priority.

That night, she decided enough was enough. She updated her résumé and began searching for new opportunities — places where her dedication to compliance would be valued. By Friday, she handed in her two-week notice. A month later, Linda started a new position at an office that welcomed her experience and passion for safety. With the dentist's support, she implemented clear systems and empowered the team with proper training. Linda thrived, knowing her work made a tangible difference.

Meanwhile, her previous practice continued to struggle with high turnover and low morale. The dentist, still plagued by inefficiency and disengagement, couldn't understand why employees didn't stay.

Linda's experience is a powerful reminder: When safety concerns are ignored, the consequences ripple through every aspect of a practice. Her emotional frustration is a feeling many dental professionals understand all too well. Being unheard, unsupported, and stuck in a practice that overlooks safety can lead to a profound sense of helplessness. Her story sheds light on some of the fears and uncertainties that can hold practices back — fear of challenging the status quo, fear of speaking up, or the belief that implementing systems is overly rigid or time-consuming.

Let's confront those fears and uncover the truths that can unlock your practice's full potential.

The Power of SYSTEM

When you think of the word SYSTEM, think of this commonly used acronym:

S – Save
Y – Your
S – Self
T – Time
E – Energy
M – Money

LIMITING BELIEFS: ADDRESSING MYTHS AND TRUTHS

Misconceptions about systems often keep practices from reaching their full potential, so it helps to understand and debunk these myths. After working with hundreds of dental practices, we've organized the most common myths into five categories. Let's confront these and uncover the truths that show how systematization can empower your team and transform your practice.

Here are some of the most common myths and why they don't hold up in the real world:

Myth 1: *Systems will make your practice rigid.*

The truth is that systems set you free.

You may fear that you could end up micromanaging your team or imposing rigid rules. But in reality, systems don't stifle creativity — they create freedom. By standardizing routine tasks, your team can focus on patient care and higher-level priorities.

Example: A simple operatory turnover checklist eliminated confusion and saved time during busy schedules. Instead of feeling restricted, the team felt empowered to work smarter and more efficiently.

Myth 2: *Systems are only for big practices.*

The truth is that systems can help small practices see big wins.

We often hear, "I run a small office — systems aren't necessary." But systems level up practices of any size. Small teams, in particular, benefit from streamlined workflows because every minute counts.

Example: When one small, six-employee office streamlined their daily workflows, it allowed them to see more patients without adding stress or extra hours.

Myth 3: If It's Working, Why Change It?

The truth is that running at the "status quo" can hide vulnerabilities.

Relying on a single team member's knowledge or habits is risky. Systems ensure consistency and protect your practice when team members leave.

Example: A thriving practice fell apart when its lead assistant retired because her knowledge hadn't been documented. Systems ensure that success isn't dependent on one person.

Myth 4: Creating Systems Takes Too Much Time

The truth is that systems are the ultimate time-saver.

Systems save countless hours by organizing what needs to be done into an easy-to-understand order, which reduces errors, improves training, and streamlines workflows.

Example: One client started small by documenting their sterilization process. The clarity and efficiency they gained inspired them to systematize the rest of their workflows, and now, they run like clockwork.

Myth 5: Employees Won't Want Systems

The truth is that employees love having clear expectations.

Most employees thrive when they know exactly what's expected of them. Systems reduce confusion, build confidence, and foster a happier work environment.

Example: One dental assistant we worked with explained how clear checklists helped her leave work without stress, knowing she had completed every task.

CHALLENGE YOUR FEARS

Now that we've discussed some of the common misconceptions holding practices back, let's reframe how we think about these doubts. Fear has a sneaky way of creeping in and making us feel stuck. But what if, instead of giving it power, we laughed at it instead?

One of my favorite pastors, Steve Backlund at Igniting Hope Ministries, has a simple, refreshing approach. When things feel difficult, he says, "Let's just laugh at that," and then literally laughs out loud. It's a reminder that fear often loses its grip when we confront it head-on and replace it with the truth. Challenging our fears — laughing at them — makes them less powerful.

Take this book, for example. I was afraid to write it. The fear told me, "What if no one reads it?" or "What if it doesn't help anyone?" But I stopped, laughed at those thoughts, and replaced them with the truth: This book will benefit many people because the knowledge shared here matters.

The same applies to you and your practice. When a fear pops up, whether it's about systems being "too rigid" or taking "too much time," I want you to pause, challenge that fear with a laugh, and replace it with the truth.

Fear: Systems are too rigid. (Ha!)

Truth: Systems give my team freedom by eliminating disorganization and guesswork.

Fear: Creating systems takes too much time. (Ha!)

Truth: The time I invest in systems now will save me countless hours later.

Laughing at fear or uncertainty removes their power. It helps you see that most doubts are unfounded and shifts your mindset from hesitation to confidence. So, the next time you catch yourself feeling stuck, try it. Laugh out loud, replace fear with the truth, and move forward with clarity and purpose.

READY FOR A CHANGE?

The powerful lesson is this: Myths are holding you back. Implementing clear systems allows your practice to create an effective, efficient workplace that gives your team the tools to succeed.

Many practices have experienced firsthand the transformation that comes with embracing change and investing in expert guidance. Here's what one of our clients shared after we helped them implement systems at their dental practice:

> *I'll admit, I was nervous at first. I thought adding systems would be complicated and make more work for us. But working with this team completely changed my perspective. They made everything so simple, and now our practice runs better than ever. I honestly can't imagine going back to the way we used to do things.*
> — DR. KATRINA MINSER, KATRINA MINSER DENTISTRY

Whoever loves discipline loves knowledge,
but whoever hates correction is unwise.
— PROVERBS 12:1 (NEW INTERNATIONAL VERSION)

Change often starts by confronting the doubts that hold us back. What are your biggest fears about implementing systems in your practice? How can you challenge those fears and turn them into truths? Let's do this together.

Step 1: Write Down Your Fears

First, list any thoughts or beliefs that make you reluctant to systematize your practice and write these in the Fear column in the table below. Some possibilities could include:

- What if my team resists these changes?
- What if it takes too much time to create systems?
- What if I fail at implementation?

Step 2: Challenge Your Fears with a Laugh

Now, read each fear aloud and then challenge it by literally laughing at it! This simple act can help release the tension around those thoughts.

Step 3: Replace Fear with Truth

In the next column, write a truth that replaces the fear. Possibilities could include:

- **Fear:** What if my team resists these changes?
- **Truth:** When employees know what's expected, they feel more confident and less stressed.
- **Fear:** What if it takes too much time to create systems?
- **Truth:** The time I invest now will save me hours of stress and mistakes later.

FEAR	TRUTH

Step 4: Commit to One Small Action

Choose one fear to address first. Commit to one small step — like drafting a checklist for operatory turnover or discussing compliance concerns with your team. Write down below what you plan to do.

_____

_____

_____

_____

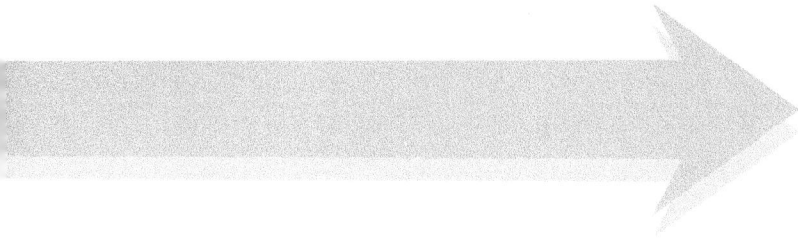

CHAPTER 4

THE SAFER PATH

True mastery lies in the ability to manage time, increase profit, and cultivate peace of mind. With the right systems, all three are within your reach.
— UNKNOWN

Many dental practices operate without written policies or procedures — not because they don't care, but because the day-to-day demands of running a practice leave little room for creating systems. In these instances, safety practices are often left to memory, on-the-go reminders, or personal interpretation, which results in inconsistency and risk.

Of the hundreds of clinics where we've worked, only about 10 percent had documented systems before working with us. The rest relied on a patchwork of unspoken rules and assumptions. This isn't just inefficient — it's dangerous for patients and staff.

The good news? Building systems doesn't have to be overwhelming. With the right guidance, you can implement processes that reduce stress, increase safety, and give your team the tools they need to thrive. Better yet, developing and following compliance systems will help you streamline operations, which ensures high standards are met and frees up time to focus on what truly matters:

providing quality care to your patients, empowering your employees to excel, and enjoying more time with family and friends outside of work.

In this chapter, we'll share *how* we approach creating dental practice systems using our SAFER Compliance Systems framework. We created this framework after years of collaborating with dentists and office managers like you. It's a practical, step-by-step approach that can help you move from responding reactively to charting a proactive course.

Even better, you'll see how compliance can be transformed from a problem you're always worried about into a possibility that enhances how you run your practice.

DO YOU BELIEVE THIS MYTH?

As we discussed in the previous chapter, "It will take too much time" is a common myth when it comes to implementing systems. We often hear clients say, "We can barely keep up with the patients we have now. We don't have time to create systems." We always want to respond, "Is that the excuse you are going to give OSHA when they show up for the inspection?" While we don't actually say that, it's what we're thinking. Let's consider the idea that you don't have time to create systems.

The Myth: I'm too busy with my patients to worry about my processes and compliance. It's just a hoop the government makes us jump through anyway.

The Truth: Creating compliance systems means a safer practice for both patients and staff. It also streamlines your workflow, allowing you to spend more time with your patients while maintaining high standards and ensuring everything stays compliant.

First, consider how systems can benefit both you and your practice. Effective systems ensure that expectations are met, patients receive excellent service, and you are prepared to tackle any challenges that arise. We visit hundreds of dental offices each year and have seen firsthand that the most successful, thriving practices all have two traits in common: clear systems and well-implemented safety programs.

These practices run smoothly, have little to no turnover, and thrive in a structured environment where everyone knows their role. Not only do these systems boost productivity and patient satisfaction, but they also ensure regulatory compliance, reduce stress and burnout for the team, and create a positive work culture. When systems are in place, everyone — from the dentist to the support staff — can focus on providing top-quality care without the distractions of inefficiencies, uncertainties, or mistakes.

These small changes could elevate your practice from average to exceptional, freeing up your time and helping you achieve results you've been too busy to pursue.

CHARTING THE SAFER PATH

Imagine a practice where safety isn't a worry, compliance is second nature, and your team operates with confidence and clarity. That's the promise of the SAFER Compliance System — a practical, step-by-step framework designed to help you systematize your practice, reduce stress, and unlock untapped potential. As a reminder, SAFER stands for Survey, Architect, Facilitate, Educate, and Review.

The SAFER Compliance System expands on the franchise approach that my mentor Frank taught me. While these foundational principles create consistency, SAFER goes further by tailoring them to the unique demands of dental compliance and adding a critical preliminary (Survey) phase.

Now, we'll explore how focusing on safety compliance can create a foundation for success. By addressing risks, standardizing processes, and empowering your team, you'll build a practice that runs efficiently, protects everyone involved, and fosters long-term growth.

Here's an illustration of the SAFER process:

SURVEY – ASSESS YOUR PRACTICE AND IDENTIFY RISKS

The first step in creating a safer, more compliant practice is understanding where you currently stand. This involves setting an operational baseline by conducting a comprehensive survey of your systems. The process is twofold — do research first and then evaluate your situation:

Research Compliance Requirements: Review all applicable laws, rules, and guidance from regulatory bodies, including OSHA, your state dental board, the

CDC, and HIPAA, as well as manufacturer Instructions for Use (IFUs) for your equipment and instruments. As you can imagine, most of these entities have a plethora of information on their websites.

Evaluate Your Facility: Walk through your practice to assess how well your current processes align with these requirements. This includes examining infection control protocols, emergency preparedness plans, and the condition of your equipment and supplies.

By systematically gathering this information, you'll uncover gaps, identify areas for improvement, and create a strong foundation for building a safer, more efficient practice.

Some Basic Recordkeeping for OSHA

OSHA requires maintaining records for compliance and workplace safety. Below are some of the basic recordkeeping requirements:

- Employee records of HBV vaccination, titer, or declination
- Employee TB testing records
- Sharps injury records – OSHA form 300
- PPE Hazard Assessment
- Updated OSHA bloodborne pathogen rules
- Electrical Hazard Assessment
- Evacuation plan
- Fire prevention plan
- Training records
- Safety Data Sheets (SDS) for all hazardous chemicals.

The Wake-up Call

Many practices unintentionally fall short by neglecting to review guidelines and device instructions. For example, manufacturer IFUs often outline specific procedures for sterilizing instruments and using equipment, but many teams rely on outdated practices, increasing risks to both patients and staff. Regular assessments ensure you're not cutting corners or introducing potential compliance violations.

Dr. Washington's wake-up call came when Carmen, the lead assistant, accidentally pricked her finger with a used anesthetic needle. Panicked, she excused herself from the patient and rushed to the sterilization room, unsure what to do. The rest of the team threw out ideas of what should happen, but there was no clear protocol to follow. "Navigating the needlestick without a direct plan was difficult, stressful, and time-consuming," Dr. Washington later recalled, "It should have been easy and straightforward, but even I didn't know the right thing to do."

This unsettling moment highlighted a critical gap in their systems: They lacked a clear plan for handling emergencies. Determined to prevent feeling this 'out of control' again, she initiated a comprehensive survey of the practice, evaluating infection control protocols, equipment maintenance, and emergency preparedness.

> *Navigating the needlestick without a direct plan was difficult, stressful, and time-consuming. It should have been easy and straightforward.*

During our assessment of the practice, the team discovered several issues, including:

- **Lack of biological indicator testing for the autoclave.** No records existed of the last spore test, leaving potential sterilization failures undetected.
- **Inconsistent waterline testing.** The team had no schedule for monitoring dental unit waterlines, leaving patients vulnerable to harmful bacteria.

- **Insufficient labeling of secondary chemical containers.** Secondary labels lacked the necessary product name and potential hazard(s), posing risks for staff.
- **No emergency action plan.** The practice lacked protocols for sharps injuries, evacuations, or natural disasters.
- **Outdated training records.** They hadn't conducted OSHA, HIPAA, or infection control training for years.

Dr. Washington was shocked to find so many hidden gaps. With this new evidence in hand, she committed to building systems to protect her patients, staff, and reputation.

Compliance doesn't end with the initial review. Staying current with updated regulations and best practices fosters a culture of continuous improvement, strengthens your team, and keeps your practice safe. Regular assessments, ongoing education, and proactive risk management safeguard your team, enhance patient care, and build resilience.

Remember: According to OSHA, "I didn't know" is not an acceptable defense. By staying informed and implementing strong systems, you create a safer, more efficient, and fully compliant environment that benefits everyone.

> *Remember: According to OSHA,*
> *"I didn't know" is not an acceptable defense.*

ARCHITECT – DOCUMENT YOUR SYSTEMS

Could you imagine a construction site without blueprints? No, because we all know that would be dangerous and lead to complete chaos. Similarly, a dental practice without documented systems leads to confusion, miscommunication, inconsistencies, and avoidable safety incidents. Step-by-step protocols serve as the foundation for a flourishing, productive team, ensuring consistency and reducing stress.

To build effective systems, follow a three-part process:

1. **Determine What Needs to Be Documented**
   Start by identifying gaps, incorrect processes, or inconsistencies uncovered during the Survey phase. This is your opportunity to address outdated or incomplete protocols and set a strong foundation for compliance and safety.

2. **Record the Steps**
   Write down every step of each process in clear, straightforward language. Consider that the person following these steps may have little or no prior experience. Include detailed instructions and photos, and ensure the steps align with manufacturer Instructions for Use (IFUs) and regulatory guidelines.

3. **Test the Steps for Clarity and Accuracy**
   Ask someone who wasn't involved in creating the protocol to follow the written steps. This ensures the instructions are easy to understand and practical for daily use. Based on their feedback, refine the document to eliminate ambiguity and improve efficiency.

Dr. Washington's Documentation Success

To prevent another incident like the needlestick, Dr. Washington worked with her team to create detailed protocols for every aspect of the practice. Starting with the needlestick procedure, they developed a step-by-step guide:

1. Stop the procedure and put the instrument in the sharps container.
2. Wash the affected area thoroughly with soap and water.

3. Notify the designated safety officer.
4. Ask the source individual (patient) to be tested.
5. Fill out the post-exposure evaluation and follow the reporting process per OSHA guidelines.
6. Send the recipient of the needlestick to be tested, preferably at an occupational health care facility. Remember, a needlestick (or sharps injury) is considered a medical emergency.

From there, they expanded their system documentation to include:

- Infection control protocols, such as sterilization procedures and documenting weekly spore testing.
- A chemical hazard communication plan with proper labeling and safety data sheets (SDS).
- Emergency action plans, including fire evacuation and natural disaster response.

By the end of this phase, every team member had access to a comprehensive safety manual, ensuring they knew exactly how to handle emergencies.

This story underscores the critical importance of documented systems. Without established systems, practices risk incidents, employee illness, and lost productivity. By investing in detailed systems, you empower your team to work cohesively, retain top talent, and ensure your practice runs smoothly.

FACILITATE – DELEGATE AND AUTOMATE

Creating clear systems is a crucial foundation. But even the best-designed systems will benefit from having the right people and tools to bring them to life. The next step is to assign clear roles, delegate responsibilities, and leverage automation to ensure your protocols are implemented effectively and consistently.

Delegate: Choose the Right Team Members

Deciding who is assigned to compliance roles is more than just filling spots; it's about choosing individuals who are knowledgeable, motivated, and organized. The following roles are essential for a compliant and safe practice:

- **Safety (OSHA) Officer:** This person oversees workplace safety, ensures compliance with OSHA standards, and coordinates safety training and audits.
- **Privacy and Security (HIPAA) Officer:** This role is responsible for protecting patient information, monitoring HIPAA compliance, and addressing potential data breaches.
- **Infection Control Coordinator (ICC):** This individual manages sterilization protocols, monitors infection prevention practices, and ensures alignment with CDC and manufacturer guidelines.

Assigning these roles to the right team members empowers them to take ownership of key compliance areas. For example, Maria, in Dr. Washington's practice, was an ideal choice for the infection control coordinator role because of her attention to detail and strong understanding of sterilization protocols.

To ensure success, provide chosen individuals with tailored training and the resources needed to excel in their roles. When roles are clearly defined and aligned with employees' strengths, your practice becomes more organized and prepared to handle compliance challenges.

Automate: Streamlining Repetitive Tasks

Automation is another key to efficiency, safety, and stress reduction. By automating repetitive tasks, your team can focus on higher-value responsibilities. Consider implementing tools to:

- Incorporate a weekly routine for spore testing and use a dedicated log or spreadsheet to record the sterilizer number, when tests were performed, the results, and whether they were sent to a lab or done in-house.
- Set up a consistent monthly or quarterly schedule for waterline testing and maintain a clear recordkeeping system to track test dates, methods (in-house or external lab), and outcomes.
- Track eyewash station flushes, fire extinguisher checks, and equipment maintenance.
- Post laminated photographs of procedural trays for visual reminders of what's needed.
- Use a texting service or patient management software to send patient appointment reminders and follow-up messages.

Putting It All Together

Effective delegation and automation work hand in hand. Assigning the right people to key compliance roles ensures your protocols are implemented correctly, while automation reduces the burden of manual processes. Together, these strategies foster a more efficient, cohesive, and productive environment where your team can thrive.

In Dr. Washington's practice, automating spore-testing schedules not only freed Maria (the infection control coordinator) from having to manually keep track of yet another task, but it also helped her catch and resolve a missed test before it became a compliance issue.

Another change Dr. Washington implemented to improve her practice was hiring a sterilization technician (sterile tech). She realized that hygienists and assistants were spending too much time on routine room cleaning and sterilizing tasks, detracting from their ability to focus on patient care. By training a dedicated sterile tech, Dr. Washington made sure that sterilization duties were handled efficiently, easing the workload on her clinical staff.

By delegating key compliance roles and adopting advanced automation tools, Dr. Washington created a strong foundation for her practice's operations. However, even the most efficient systems and tools are only as effective as the people using them.

To ensure success, teams need proper training to understand their responsibilities, implement protocols, and stay aligned with regulatory standards.

That's why education is the next critical step in transforming a practice.

EDUCATE – EMPOWER YOUR TEAM

Training your team is a cornerstone of compliance and safety. Regular education ensures your staff is confident, competent, and aligned with your practice's standards and regulatory requirements.

Training is essential at multiple points:

- onboarding new hires
- introducing new activities
- learning new devices
- implementing system changes
- providing annual, all-team refreshers

Dr. Washington's Team Training Plan

After delegating key compliance roles and implementing automation, Dr. Washington recognized that her team needed proper training to fully leverage these changes. She scheduled a comprehensive compliance training that covered OSHA, HIPAA, and infection control guidelines.

During ongoing safety and infection control meetings, the team focused on more specific activities, including responding to needlestick injuries, a critical gap uncovered during the survey phase. The team practiced the new protocol step by step, ensuring everyone understood their roles. Carmen shared her experience from the initial incident: "At the time, I didn't know what to do, and it was terrifying. Now, I feel better because we all know what to do."

Throughout the year, they held regular safety meetings that included reviews of protocols and hands-on activities such as mock emergency drills. These exercises not only strengthened the team's knowledge but also boosted their confidence and collaboration.

As the newly appointed infection control coordinator, Maria introduced monthly safety quizzes as a fun and engaging way to keep compliance top of mind. Jared, the privacy officer, led a segment on protecting patient data, emphasizing simple steps like avoiding phishing scams by not clicking email links.

By prioritizing training, Dr. Washington's team grew more confident, collaborative, and prepared for any challenge. Comprehensive, ongoing education fosters a culture of improvement, keeping staff engaged and your practice compliant.

Beyond compliance, training fosters a culture of continuous improvement. Regular workshops, team refreshers, and ongoing education keep staff engaged and aligned with best practices. Partnering with external compliance training resources ensures your programs remain current and efficient.

Education lays the groundwork for a skilled and confident team, but maintaining excellence requires ongoing monitoring. Regular reviews and audits ensure that systems stay effective and your team remains compliant with the latest standards.

REVIEW – USE LOGS AND AUDITS TO ENSURE SUCCESS

Once systems are set up and operations are running smoothly, you're on your way, but you're not quite done. To keep systems operating efficiently, you'll need to conduct regular reviews and audits to ensure that they remain effective and compliant.

For example, reviewing compliance logs (such as those for flushing eyewash stations, degassing the ultrasonic, or cleaning dental amalgam filters) creates a record of accountability. Logs document completed tasks with dates and initials, providing a clear framework for spotting and addressing discrepancies before they escalate into bigger issues.

Audits serve as a feedback loop to verify that processes remain aligned with current standards. Think of your standard operating procedures (SOPs) as living documents that evolve alongside your practice. Frequent reviews make all the difference in identifying gaps and ensuring continuous improvement.

Steps for an Effective Audit

A successful audit involves four key steps:

1. **Plan the Audit:** Identify the areas or systems to review, set objectives, and decide who will conduct the audit. Use checklists or templates to ensure nothing is overlooked.
2. **Perform the Audit:** Examine logs, observe procedures, and collect data to evaluate compliance with established protocols. Engage team members to clarify processes and address immediate questions.
3. **Analyze the Audit Results:** Compare findings against standards and identify gaps or inconsistencies. Highlight successes as well as areas needing improvement.
4. **Adapt Based on the Audit:** Share findings with the team, adjust systems or procedures, and provide additional training if necessary. Use the results to refine your SOPs and reinforce accountability.

Dr. Washington's Audit Success Story

After implementing the systems in her practice, Dr. Washington introduced a schedule of regular audits to ensure her team's hard work would continue paying off. One of her first audits focused on infection control practices, where she reviewed sterilization logs, waterline testing records, and ultrasonic and autoclave maintenance.

During this audit, Maria, the infection control coordinator, noticed a gap: Spore testing wasn't being conducted consistently, with some team members forgetting to document weekly tests. Instead of assigning blame, Dr. Washington used the findings as a teaching moment. She worked with the team to create a color-coding checklist to make the process easier to track.

Dr. Washington also conducted a hand hygiene audit using a simple spreadsheet to track compliance before, during, and after patient care. The results revealed that many staff members were skipping critical steps. Sharing these findings during a safety meeting turned the process into a collaborative effort, with the team rallying around the opportunity to improve. Within a few months, their performance had drastically improved, earning them recognition and a celebratory team lunch.

Frequent reviews and audits do more than meet regulatory requirements; they foster accountability, mindfulness, and a culture of continuous improvement. By regularly monitoring and refining your systems, you can maintain excellence, retain top-performing staff, and ensure your practice aligns with compliance standards and long-term goals. As Dr. Washington discovered, audits aren't just about catching mistakes; they're about empowering your team to strive for excellence every day.

TALK WITH EXPERTS TO SIMPLIFY YOUR PROCESS

If all of this feels overwhelming, don't worry. You don't have to go it alone. Working with a compliance company can make the entire process easier and give you confidence that your systems support your needs and match evolving regulations.

Look for companies that offer:

- Customizable SOPs tailored to your unique needs.
- State-specific expertise for compliance with local regulations.
- Ongoing support for questions, updates, and troubleshooting.
- Comprehensive assessments to identify risks and provide actionable solutions.
- Engaging training that your team actually enjoys and learns from.

With the right partner, you can simplify compliance, save time, and gain confidence knowing your practice is secure. A trusted partner acts as an extension of your team, helping you focus on what matters most: patient care.

YOU'RE ALREADY EQUIPPED

You might still be wondering whether systematizing compliance is possible for your practice. Let me assure you: You can do this. You've already successfully completed dental school, built a practice, and handled countless other challenges along the way. Creating a system that makes your practice more efficient and your life easier is well within your reach.

Systematizing compliance isn't about perfection — it's about progress. Small, consistent steps can lead to monumental changes. The SAFER process is straightforward, achievable, and results-driven — designed for busy professionals like you. You don't have to figure it all out at once; just take the first step, and momentum will carry you forward.

> *Systematizing compliance*
> *isn't about perfection —*
> *it's about progress.*

Picture This

Imagine walking into your practice with confidence, knowing that everything is running smoothly and meeting your expectations. Your employees easily navigate their day, and your patients feel cared for and appreciated, driving growth and retention. This isn't a fantasy — it's your reality with the SAFER model.

Let's address a common concern — that this is another cookie-cutter, one-size-fits-all compliance program. It is not. The SAFER process is not built around generic guidelines and will not overwhelm you with unnecessary complexity. And it certainly won't require you to dedicate endless hours reinventing the wheel.

What this approach offers is a proven, practical solution tailored to your practice's unique needs. You'll get detailed guidance, step-by-step systems, and personalized solutions that simplify compliance, streamline operations, and build a safer, happier workplace. It's logical, efficient, and designed with you in mind.

Are you ready to take the first step toward transforming your practice? Let's make it happen.

> *The time to repair your roof is when the sun is shining.*
> — JOHN F. KENNEDY

Compliance is the foundation of a safe, efficient, and thriving practice. Each step of the SAFER framework moves you toward an effective system. Here, we're going to focus on getting started by starting the **Survey** process. It's meant to help you identify where your practice currently stands and where improvements are needed. By taking a proactive approach, you can build a strong foundation that ensures safety, consistency, and peace of mind.

To make this process simple and actionable, we've created a quick, easy-to-use **OSHA Compliance Checklist**. This tool guides you through essential safety standards and highlights foundational compliance tasks that improve both operations and workflows. Think of it as your starting point for creating a safer and more efficient practice.

Here's how to get started:

1. **Get the checklist**. Visit GoodDentistBook.com to download the OSHA Compliance Checklist.

2. **Conduct a walkthrough**. Use the OSHA checklist to walk through your practice. Check off the tasks you're currently meeting and circle the areas where improvements are needed.

3. **Prioritize actions**. Choose 1-3 circled items to focus on this month. Start with the areas that pose the greatest safety risk or create the most inefficiency.

Expert Tip

Involve your team in the walkthrough. Their insights can reveal issues you may not have noticed. Engaging the team in the process brings in their expertise and builds a culture of safety and accountability.

Taking this first step will not only clarify your current compliance status but also set you on the path to creating a stronger, safer, and more organized practice. Remember, every small improvement moves you closer to a thriving practice.

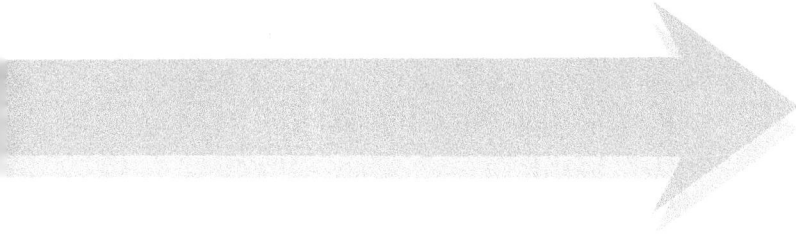

CHAPTER 5

START WITH THE BASICS

Small changes can create big wins.
— ANONYMOUS

Have you ever ordered your favorite meal at a restaurant, only to find it doesn't taste the same as usual? Inconsistency at a restaurant is disappointing. Inconsistency at a dental practice is dangerous for your patients and your staff. Without written systems, staff can default to doing things their own way, potentially skipping critical steps or relying on outdated practices.

In this chapter, we're going to apply our SAFER framework to common dental practice challenges. You'll see how our Survey - Architect - Facilitate - Educate - Review framework can be used to improve consistency, accountability, and safety.

THE CONVERSATION THAT CHANGED EVERYTHING

When onboarding new clients, we spend time talking with them to see what outcomes they'd like to see. When we started working with Transform

Dentistry, they wanted help establishing effective infection control systems for their instrument reprocessing. Dr. Stanford was a new practice owner and was committed to doing right by his team, patients, and practice. During our first visit, we met with Kayla, the office's lead assistant, to discuss her concerns.

"Some of our staff rush through the process and pull instruments out of the autoclave as soon as the door opens, skipping the drying cycle," she explained, obviously frustrated.

Kayla was right to be concerned. Skipping the drying cycle isn't just a minor shortcut; it jeopardizes patient safety and reduces the life of instruments.

Expert Tip

Bacteria and Germs Thrive in Moisture. If instruments aren't completely dry, any remaining moisture creates the perfect environment for bacteria and germs to grow. This means instruments that were sterilized can become contaminated again before use.

Damage to Instruments. Moisture left on instruments can cause corrosion or damage over time, which reduces their lifespan and effectiveness, leading to costly replacements.

Follow the Instructions

From assembling a bookshelf to making a batch of chocolate chip cookies, it's important to follow the provided instructions to complete the task properly. Doing so delivers reliable, consistent results. This is no accident. Teams of testers have reviewed and revised the instructions until only the best, most foolproof version is agreed upon and given to customers.

However, if users skip steps or substitute ingredients, their results won't match expectations. The same principle applies in dentistry. Manufacturers rigorously test the safest, most effective ways to use their instruments, devices, and products. The resulting guidelines, called Instructions for Use (IFUs), are essential to ensure safety and the proper use of devices. Failing to review and follow these instructions can lead to inconsistencies that put patients, staff, and equipment at risk.

SURVEY YOUR SITUATION

Imagine running your dental practice without a written schedule. Everything would fall apart — appointments would overlap, patients would be frustrated by delays, and staff would be scrambling to figure out where to be and what to do. The same is true for your systems and processes: Without written documentation, tasks become inconsistent, errors are more likely, and accountability is impossible.

Establishing proper systems begins with the Survey phase (the "S" in SAFER), where you evaluate current practices to uncover hidden gaps and inconsistencies. This includes reviewing protocols, observing workflows, and understanding how the team operates. These insights form the foundation for improvement by identifying inconsistencies and missing protocols that need to be addressed.

But uncovering gaps is just the start. The next step, Architect (the "A" in SAFER), involves translating those findings into clear, written systems. Documenting and standardizing protocols creates a roadmap for consistency, safety, and accountability across your team.

At Transform Dental, we spent a few hours reviewing their documentation, observing the team, and asking pointed questions. One key finding was that some staff members were cutting corners, such as skipping the drying cycle during instrument sterilization. This critical step, outlined in the equipment's Instructions for Use (IFUs), ensures that instruments remain sterile and free from contamination. Overlooking it jeopardizes both patient safety and the lifespan of the instruments. Consequently, we created a comprehensive sterilization protocol based on their equipment's specific IFU guidelines and government regulations. The protocol clearly documented every step of the process — from cleaning to drying. The written system was augmented with photos and then reinforced during interactive training sessions. To help with daily adherence, we also implemented a checklist to verify that each task was completed after every cycle.

After giving Kayla the protocols, she sighed with relief and admitted, "These are great because up until now, everyone has done things their own way."

A couple of weeks later, we called Kayla to check in. Her voice was chipper as she shared, "Now, everyone is on the same page. I can already see the difference in how the team works together."

This transformation highlights how compliance systems can turn frustration and uncertainty into confidence and consistency, creating a safer environment and a more cohesive team.

Without clear, written protocols, employees often fall back on what they learned years ago — or worse, make up their own methods. This inconsistency can have serious consequences, including ambiguity in processes, risky shortcuts, and the danger of spreading infections and illnesses.

Documented systems remove ambiguity, minimize errors, and establish accountability. When a team member deviates from the process, leadership can address the issue constructively by referring to the written standard. This approach eliminates subjectivity, reinforces professionalism, and fosters reliability across the team.

Creating simple, clear systems, like SOPs, brings order and reliability to your practice. These documented systems eliminate uncertainty, reduce errors, and ensure tasks are completed consistently every time.

DOCUMENT LIKE A PRO

After surveying what processes are in place and identifying what protocols are needed (the "S" in SAFER), it's time to architect and document systems (the "A" in SAFER). While creating written documentation may seem daunting, our step-by-step SAFER framework makes the process manageable and collaborative. Think of the phrase "Divide and conquer!" It perfectly applies to developing systems.

We recommend working with your team to design your protocols. First, identify who the go-to experts are on your team. Every office has staff members who excel at certain tasks — they're the people everyone turns to with questions on technical issues.

Then, select someone else to be the "documenter." We recommend that the assigned documenter be detail-oriented and skilled at organizing information. This person will pair with the process expert and will write out the expert's knowledge in a step-by-step manner. This buddy system fosters teamwork, ensures accuracy, and makes documentation a more engaging activity.

Now that your team is in place, you can begin the SAFER process of documenting protocols. We like to structure it as follows:

- The documenter shadows the expert in action, carefully watching them perform a task step-by-step.
- While writing down what happens, the documenter asks clarifying questions along the way to ensure points are fully understood and nothing is overlooked.
- Together, the pair reviews every detail, including important steps, tools, and potential pitfalls.

We also recommend including photos of equipment, devices, and/or setups for even greater clarity. Visuals like these can help eliminate confusion and make the instructions more user-friendly.

Expert Tip

Take photos of tray setups for specific procedures to save time and eliminate confusion. With clear visual references, there's no guesswork about which instruments are required. These photos serve as quick guides for all team members, from seasoned employees to those less familiar with certain procedures.

This simple strategy ensures consistency, reduces stress, and boosts efficiency. Employees can prepare trays confidently, allowing the team to focus on patient care without unnecessary delays. Trays will be assembled the same way every time, eliminating questions and interruptions so your team can concentrate on other important activities.

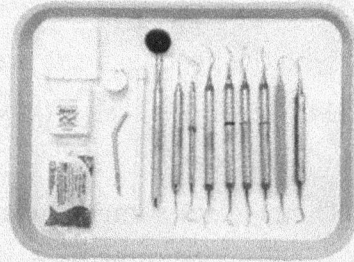

Leverage Technology

For maximum efficiency, we suggest leveraging technology to format, organize, and share your documentation. Start by using a standardized template to ensure all SOPs are consistent, clear, and easy to follow. Templates save time, prevent omissions, and provide a professional structure that supports onboarding and daily operations.

To ensure the ongoing maintenance of these systems, consider using a simple spreadsheet or investing in SOP software. This links directly to each specific SOP and will help you track and monitor revisions as well as document training completion. By providing a central location for all systems, your team can easily access the most up-to-date information when they need it.

This system not only keeps your team aligned with updated protocols but also ensures accountability and consistency across the practice. With everything in one place, maintaining compliance becomes more efficient and less time-consuming.

You don't have to reinvent the wheel — download a free, ready-to-use digital SOP template at GoodDentistBook.com. These templates will help you focus on what matters most: creating systems that work for your practice.

> *Using a template made the entire process so much easier.*
> *I didn't have to start from scratch, and the prompts ensured*
> *I didn't miss anything important. My team appreciated*
> *having everything laid out clearly — it's been a*
> *game-changer for onboarding and daily operations.*
> **— DR. LILLIAN VOSS**

Test and Refine

Once the initial draft of your SOP is complete, it's time to test it. This is the third part of the Architect step in the SAFER framework. Ask another team member to follow the instructions exactly as written. This step ensures the process is clear and practical for someone who wasn't involved in creating it.

If they encounter any confusion or roadblocks, refine the SOP based on their feedback. Encourage team members to suggest improvements and highlight ways to make the workflow even smoother. This collaborative approach not only ensures the SOP reflects the most efficient process but also fosters a sense of ownership among staff.

Testing your SOP isn't just about finding errors; it's an opportunity to build team engagement. When staff members see their feedback integrated into protocols, they're more likely to follow and respect the system.

THE POWER OF CLEAR SYSTEMS

Developing SOPs is an investment in your team, practice, and patient safety. By documenting processes in a clear and consistent format, you eliminate uncertainty, minimize errors, and ensure accountability across all levels.

Detailed checklists and regular training make it easier for staff to follow protocols and for managers to ensure compliance. When your team sees how these systems simplify their work, their morale improves, and adherence becomes second nature.

Why It Matters

Well-documented systems don't just meet compliance standards; they create a smoother, more reliable practice. Small changes — like ensuring adherence to manufacturer instructions or standardizing workflows — lead to big improvements in safety, efficiency, and teamwork. By addressing inconsistencies, you protect both your team and your patients while building a stronger practice.

Starting small and involving your team can transform your practice into a model of clarity and organization. With each new system you develop, you'll be building a safer, more efficient environment that benefits everyone.

> *The real power of a system is that it gives you freedom.*
> — T. HARV EKER

CREATE YOUR FIRST SOP

Standard operating procedures (SOPs) ensure consistency and safety in every dental practice. Most offices have 25 to 50 SOPs covering essential areas like sterilization, chemical safety, and emergency protocols.

In this section, you'll learn how to create your first SOP for instrument sterilization, laying the groundwork for building a comprehensive system for your practice.

Step 1: Locate Your Instructions for Use (IFU)

- *Locate (or look online for) the IFU for your autoclave, STATIM, or other sterilization devices you use.*
- *Remember to always to keep IFUs near each device for easy access.*

Step 2: Gather Your Clinical Team

- *Call a clinical team meeting. Explain that this is a collaborative exercise to ensure everyone understands the process and works consistently.*
- *Set the tone for transparency and collaboration: "We're going to walk through the instructions for operating this device together. If you notice anything we're doing differently, or if a step feels unclear, speak up. This isn't about blame but ensuring we're all on the same page."*

Step 3: Review and Compare Instructions Together

- *Read the IFU step by step, out loud. Focus on the sections about operation, cleaning, and maintenance.*
- *Pause after each step to ask:*
  - *"Is this how we're currently doing it?" If not, ask, "Why?"*
  - *"Are there any differences between the instructions and our actual process?"*

Step 4: Identify Gaps and Plan Corrections.

- *As you go through the IFU, assign someone who is detail-oriented to write each step in a clear, simple list.*
- *Take photos of equipment, buttons, or specific setups to include alongside your notes.*

Step 5: Turn the Exercise into a Documented System

Once you've created your first written procedure, test it:

- *Have another team member follow the steps without extra guidance. Can they complete the task without confusion?*
- *Refine it. Adjust any unclear steps or gaps based on feedback.*

This exercise is a great starting point, but if you're feeling unsure about documenting processes or aligning your team, we can help. At HCA, we'll work with you to streamline workflows and make compliance easy. Visit GoodDentistBook.com for more information.

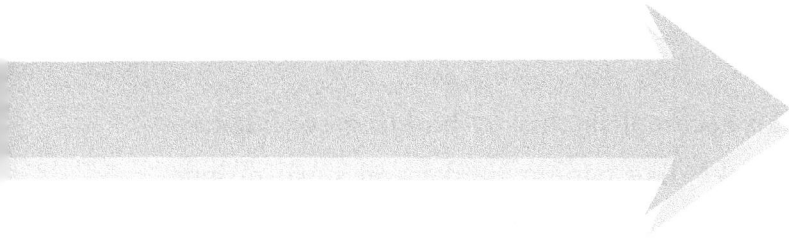

CHAPTER 6

HAPPY EMPLOYEES

Systems allow ordinary people to achieve extraordinary results predictably.
— MICHAEL GERBER

Dentists often assume that implementing procedures and systems will be perceived negatively by their employees. They worry that "too many rules" will make staff think they aren't trusted to make decisions. But the opposite is true. When specific processes are put in place, employees know exactly what is expected and how it should be accomplished. This provides a host of benefits to the practice. It streamlines both the training of existing staff and the onboarding of new hires. Most importantly, it results in employees feeling empowered and in control, which leads to greater job satisfaction and contentment — factors essential for a successful practice.

Additionally, there has been a cultural shift in the workplace. Today's dental teams expect more than just a paycheck — they want to feel valued, supported, and part of a collaborative environment. Practices with this type of office culture can lower turnover, boost morale, and foster motivated, high-performing teams.

Clear training and processes can accomplish this by building confidence. Step-by-step instructions for daily tasks (like patient intake and sterilization) eliminate confusion, reduce mistakes, and improve employee satisfaction. Practices that include staff in creating systems foster a sense of ownership and collaboration. A part-time hygienist shared, "Being part of developing our morning checklist made me feel like I had a say in how we work as a team."

Effective processes can also help practices meet the growing demand for an improved work-life balance. Employees thrive in workplaces where clear systems and job expectations allow them to leave work on time without stress. One dental assistant explained, "Before, I felt guilty leaving because I wasn't sure I'd done everything I was supposed to. Now, with checklists, I leave knowing I've completed my tasks."

Prioritizing employee growth also strengthens commitment. Regular training, cross-training, and collaborative team meetings not only improve skills but also show employees they're valued. A hygienist said, "Mini-trainings during team meetings make me feel like I'm growing instead of just doing the same thing every day."

PEOPLE THRIVE INSIDE SYSTEMS

Humans are wired to seek predictability. Clear, documented systems reduce uncertainty, allowing team members to focus on their work instead of feeling unsure about what comes next. When employees know exactly what's expected of them, they feel more confident and less stressed, which leads to fewer mistakes, higher productivity, and greater job satisfaction.

> *When employees know exactly what's expected of them, they feel more confident and less stressed, which leads to fewer mistakes, higher productivity, and greater job satisfaction.*

As a teacher, to keep the classroom running smoothly, it was important to develop routines and systems for everything. For example, when it came time to turn in homework, chaos could easily erupt if all the students got up at once to take their papers to the inbox. To solve this, I created a simple system — releasing students by row.

Students in the first row would stand, walk to the inbox, and then return to their seats following a designated path. After the last student in that row had passed, the students in the next row would stand and proceed to the inbox. This staggered approach created a clear flow, eliminated bottlenecks, and kept the process calm and efficient. It also helped students stay focused and reduced unnecessary distractions. It not only ensured the task got done but also instilled a sense of order and responsibility in the students. Even small systems can have a big impact on creating a productive environment.

While systems, of course, create order, they also send a message to your team: "We value your time and effort." This fosters a culture of trust and teamwork, where every employee feels supported and motivated to perform their best. The result? A practice that runs more efficiently and a team that thrives together.

A STRESS-FREE SOLUTION FOR NEW HIRES

Clear systems also reduce the anxiety and disruption that often occur when bringing a new employee up to speed. Dr. Lillian Voss learned firsthand the value of these systems after creating processes for her busy practice.

Before they implemented their current systems, onboarding new employees was like gathering leaves on a windy day. Every new hire meant starting from scratch, juggling a whirlwind of tasks — paperwork, training, and hands-on instruction — on top of her regular duties. Without a clear process, mistakes were common, new employees felt unsupported, and existing employees were overwhelmed.

The onboarding process wasn't working, and Dr. Lillian was determined to make a change. She talked to Melissa, her office manager, and said, "We can't keep doing this. We've got SOPs for other things. Why don't we have one for this?"

The next day, Melissa began documenting systems for their HR paperwork while Dr. Lillian outlined the specific steps they needed to take to train the new hires for clinical work. Recording their methods proved to be invaluable, enabling reflection on past practices and identifying safer, more efficient approaches. They created a comprehensive training program that included step-by-step instructions, photos, and checklists covering everything from filling out W-4 forms to hands-on patient care training. As a result, every new hire had a roadmap that guided them in their roles.

The impact was immediate. The next time they hired a new team member, Melissa noticed the difference. "In just two days, my onboarding tasks are nearly complete — it used to take weeks!"

Dr. Lillian agreed, "Clinical training is much better, too. I walked her through the steps using the SOPs, and she's doing great."

At her three-month check-in, the new hire couldn't contain her excitement. "I've never had such a great experience with a new job. The SOPs make communication so easy, and I don't need to keep bothering you with questions!"

Dr. Lillian felt proud to be the boss she always wanted to be.

An Unexpected Benefit

In today's challenging staffing environment, documented systems provided another major advantage for Dr. Lillian's clinic: **the ability to seamlessly hire temporary employees**.

Before they had documented systems, hiring a temp was a stressful, chaotic experience. On one such occasion, Dr. Lillian's lead assistant called in sick on a Sunday evening. With a full schedule the next day, including two crown procedures, Dr. Lillian scrambled to find a replacement. She left a message with a dental staffing agency, feeling anxious about the day ahead.

The agency called Monday morning to confirm they were sending someone over. Dr. Lillian felt a wave of relief — but also a deep sense of dread. She knew training a temp on the fly would eat into her packed schedule.

That day, the temp assistant held suction during procedures but wasn't familiar with the clinic's flow or protocols. Between patients, Dr. Lillian rushed to guide the temp on instrument processing. At the end of each visit, she had to document charts herself because the temp didn't know how to navigate their system.

By the day's end, Dr. Lillian felt like she had sprinted a marathon. While she managed to keep the clinic running, the inefficiency and stress left her exhausted and frustrated.

Now, with the systems binder in place, hiring a temp is a completely different experience. Temps can easily refer to the binder to look up protocols, understand patient flow, and assist with specific procedures.

"It's made everything so much easier," Dr. Lillian said, relieved. "I can maintain my day's pace without carrying the extra load of training or picking up the slack."

RETHINKING YOUR STRATEGIES

In dental practices, common training and staffing strategies — like shadowing, relying solely on skilled hires, or randomly assigning compliance roles — may seem effective at first glance. However, these approaches often fail to address long-term challenges, leading to inconsistencies, inefficiencies, and burnout.

In order to create a sustainable, efficient practice, it's essential to recognize the limitations of these traditional methods and embrace systems that foster consistency, accountability, and growth. Let's explore some of the shortcomings of these outdated strategies and why structured systems are the key to success.

Shadowing is Not a Long-term Strategy

The industry has relied on methods like shadowing for a long time. Watching someone else work might give new hires a general idea of what's expected, but it doesn't explain each step and why it's required.

By not providing details and specifics, shadowing does not effectively standardize daily tasks, leaving new hires with a patchwork of processes instead of clear, cohesive systems. This approach can cause confusion and inefficiencies, especially in high-stakes areas like sterilization protocols and dental procedures.

Shadowing also burdens experienced staff, adding to their already busy workload and forcing them to divide their attention between training and completing assigned tasks. This can result in missed details and frustration on both sides. And shadowing depends heavily on the skills, habits, and teaching style of the person being shadowed. If the trainer skips steps or cuts corners, then the new hire is likely to adopt those same behaviors, creating gaps in performance and compliance.

Even worse, shadowing doesn't give new hires a reliable guide they can refer back to after their initial training ends. New employees are left relying on memory, which increases the likelihood of mistakes and slows productivity.

Without clear, written processes, it's challenging to hold anyone accountable for errors since there's no standard to measure against. Transitioning from shadowing to documented systems solves these issues by providing consistent, clear instructions that can be easily followed and referenced.

Systems ensure tasks are performed the same way every time, reduce the burden on trainers, and give new hires the confidence to succeed independently. Documented systems foster accountability, improve efficiency, and eliminate the guesswork, creating a smoother, more reliable training experience for everyone.

Hiring Skilled Labor is Not Your Only Option

When building your team, it might seem logical to focus on hiring employees who already have the required skills and training. While this can be an advantage, it raises an important question: Do these employees have the skills and training to perform the job the way *you* want it done?

Many practices have found success by hiring non-skilled workers whose work ethic aligns with the team and then training them on the practice's established systems. These employees come with a fresh perspective, unencumbered by preconceived notions of how things "should" be done. This makes it easier to teach them the practice's unique workflows and expectations. Employees who receive thoughtful, in-house training can often feel more invested in the practice because of the time and effort spent on their development.

Let's say you hire a new sterile tech with no prior experience. After a quick tutorial, this employee can confidently perform essential tasks like room turnover with the documented systems you've designed. SOPs provide a roadmap, allowing even less experienced staff to execute their responsibilities consistently and efficiently.

Of course, roles like hygienists and high-level assistants require specific licensing and credentials. However, the idea of using SOPs as roadmaps applies across all positions: **Systems are the great equalizer**. They provide structure, eliminate confusion, and empower team members to work together effectively. By prioritizing systems, your practice operates at its best and creates an environment where every employee feels capable, confident, and motivated to contribute to the team's success.

Expert HR Tip

SOPs become your written policy for employee expectations. If an employee is not following the protocol, it is easy to refer them back to the SOP and offer additional training if needed.

CHOOSING COMPLIANCE ROLES

After establishing SOPs to streamline operations, it's time to identify the individuals who will oversee and manage your practice's compliance needs. These folks are important. The individuals assigned to compliance roles do more than just fill a spot. They provide a critical service by maintaining a compliant and safe practice. This is the "F" — facilitating step — of the SAFER model. They review and manage daily operations to ensure the systems are running smoothly.

Compliance roles that need to be covered at every office include:

- Safety (OSHA) Officer
- Privacy and Security (HIPAA) Officer
- Infection Control Coordinator (ICC)

In smaller clinics, these roles may overlap. For every office, we recommend appointing a secondary person to assist and serve as backup. This ensures continuity and shared responsibility, especially during busy periods or staff absences. For an outline of how to select the right team member for your officers, visit GoodDentistBook.com.

Selection Process

When choosing leaders for these roles, focus on employees who naturally gravitate toward following protocols and upholding safety standards. Often, those who identify as rule-followers or who take pride in meticulous work make excellent candidates. These individuals bring a level of consistency and detail necessary to manage compliance effectively.

It's important to keep in mind that these roles come with additional responsibilities. Expecting someone to fit compliance tasks into an already busy schedule can lead to frustration and burnout. Instead, allocate dedicated time in their work week specifically for these duties and consider offering a raise or stipend to recognize the extra responsibilities. This will reinforce the significance of their role and ensure they have enough capacity to perform well.

Jeanine, the safety officer and lead dental assistant at Giever Orthodontics, demonstrates the importance of choosing the right person for the role and providing proper support. Dr. Giever, who saw compliance as more of a nuisance than a necessity, rarely engaged with the practice's training or systems. One day, while reviewing paperwork, he noticed the annual invoice for compliance services and asked Jeanine, "We pay this every year; is it worth it?"

Jeanine didn't hesitate, "Yes!" she replied emphatically, "I wouldn't continue being the safety officer without their support."

Her response speaks volumes about the value and complexity of the safety officer role. It's not just about walking through the office once a year and checking boxes. Doing a safety officer role correctly requires time, focus, and commitment to ensure the safety and compliance of the entire practice.

Safety officers and infection control coordinators (ICCs) have a significant responsibility to keep the practice compliant and safe. Their primary expertise may be dentistry, but when given the right support, they can successfully navigate the nuances of compliance.

Supporting employee training and providing resources is the "E" (educate) in the SAFER Compliance System. Employees value growth opportunities, and training creates a culture of continuous improvement. Activities like workshops, team updates, and ongoing education make staff more likely to stay engaged and committed, resulting in a practice that runs cohesively.

ESTABLISHING STANDARDS

While clear processes provide the roadmap for success, employees can quickly become dissatisfied and unmotivated if they sense that not everyone is following systems or being held to the same standards. Accountability ensures everyone stays on course. Without it, even the best-documented systems can falter. This is the "R" — review step — of the SAFER model.

Our company experienced firsthand the critical importance of enforcing standards. Our team was facing a recurring issue with a long-time employee, Tera. She was resistant to the systems we had worked so hard to implement and often grumbled, "We didn't do it this way before." Needless to say, her performance repeatedly fell short of expectations.

Our operations manager, Ayana, grew increasingly frustrated after yet another client complained. "Tera skipped key steps again," she said. "The client was confused and wants a different consultant."

I knew avoiding conflict was not an option. To handle this properly, I contacted the Bureau of Labor and Industries (BOLI) for guidance. Their advice was simple yet powerful: **"Document everything. Make your expectations clear, and track whether employees follow them."**

During the next staff meeting, we revisited our SOPs, reminding everyone of the standards we expected. Then, we introduced regular audits to ensure accountability.

The data quickly showed a pattern. Tera's noncompliance was off the charts, even with extra coaching. When I called her in to discuss the results, I felt confident in my decision to let her go. Despite her initial accusations of unfair treatment, I had documentation that showed our standards and how they were applied equally to everyone.

While letting Tera go wasn't an easy decision, it was the right one. As a business owner, I felt an overwhelming sense of relief knowing that every member of my team was meeting expectations, supporting our clients, and working cohesively. What made it even more reassuring was the unanimous support and gratitude from the team. We were completely aligned, united by a shared vision of excellence and a renewed sense of purpose.

This experience illustrates the value of audits and clear systems and how they can help maintain fairness and ensure success. **Regular reviews catch small**

issues early, prevent major disruptions, and create a sense of accountability that benefits everyone.

Recognize and Motivate Employees

Everyone appreciates being recognized. Here are some possibilities:

- **Appreciation Box** — Create a place for team members where they can anonymously recognize each other for following systems, solving problems, or going the extra mile. Read during team meetings.
- **Incentive Program** — Create a reward system for employees who consistently follow documented systems, such as points redeemable for gift cards, a bonus, or a special team lunch.
- **Team Celebration Jar** — Encourage employees to celebrate the small wins by jotting down how systems helped them succeed or reduce stress. Share wins monthly over coffee, snacks, or lunch.
- **Milestone Rewards** — Celebrate system milestones (e.g., completing sterilization logs or passing an audit) with small rewards.

Schedule Check-Ins

Even the most well-thought-out systems can falter without regular review and adjustments (the "R" in SAFER). This is where quarterly check-ins become invaluable. They provide a structured opportunity to evaluate progress, ensure alignment with compliance protocols, and support team development.

Regularly scheduled check-ins allow you to create a consistent feedback loop. Employees are encouraged to assess their own performance while management provides objective evaluations using clear, predefined criteria. During these meetings, metrics like adherence to compliance protocols (based on audits), contributions to team efficiency, and feedback from patients or coworkers can be reviewed. This data-based approach promotes transparency and helps identify areas that need improvement.

Expert Tip

Internal chat software such as Microsoft Teams (or Slack) can be used to document communication, corrections, and warnings with employees. Teams Chat keeps track of ALL internal communications with individuals and groups and can be easily searched and referenced. This system is far more efficient than attempting to send and manage emails! It's also really easy to set up and use.

These check-ins are also an opportunity to address any challenges or bottlenecks that may arise. For instance, if a new hire struggles with adapting to different systems or if a compliance officer feels overwhelmed, the quarterly review offers a safe space to discuss solutions and clarify expectations.

Perhaps most importantly, check-ins offer the opportunity to celebrate successes. Recognizing team members who excel at following procedures or who contribute innovative ideas reinforces positive behaviors and boosts morale. When employees are acknowledged and supported, it helps them feel valued and encourages long-term commitment.

My staff feels more confident knowing we took action to solve everyday workplace problems. This has created a positive environment where employees feel supported and valued.
— DR. BRIAN STANFORD, TRANSFORM DENTISTRY

Continuous improvement is better than delayed perfection.
— MARK TWAIN

Help Others Discover Their Journey to Success

There's a meaningful way to help other dental professionals without spending a dime.

Here's a question for you: Would you lend a hand to someone who could use your guidance if it only took a few seconds and didn't cost you anything?

If so, here's how. There are dental professionals and practice managers out there facing the same challenges you're working to solve. By leaving an honest review, you'll give them insight into how this book could make a difference in their practice. It might be just what they need to take that next step toward a smoother, more successful business.

Your honest feedback will take less than a minute.

Thank you for sharing this journey with me and for taking a moment to help others who are seeking the same peace of mind and practical solutions you've discovered. Your words could be the encouragement someone else needs to get started.

TAKE ACTION: CREATE YOUR ONBOARDING CHECKLIST

Creating a streamlined onboarding process doesn't have to be overwhelming. Start by jotting down every step you take when hiring and training a new employee. Consider what information they need to succeed from day one, such as essential paperwork, clinic protocols, and clinical training steps. Then, organize these steps sequentially in the order they should happen.

Instructions:

1. Write down each task in the Task column.
2. Use the Order column to assign the sequence (1 for first, 2 for second, etc.).
3. Share with your office manager and clarify any additional steps.
4. Create a clean copy of this document as a checklist.

Onboarding Checklist

TASK	ORDER

To make it even easier, we've created a free, customizable employee onboarding checklist. This resource will save you time, reduce stress, and ensure your new hires feel confident and supported from the start.

Download your free onboarding checklist today! Visit GoodDentistBook.com now.

Expert Tip

Create a single location (a hard copy or digital folder) where all the forms needed for onboarding a new hire are kept.

CHAPTER 7

THE POWER OF EFFICIENCY

Time is the one resource we can't create more of —
master your schedule, and you master your success.
— UNKNOWN

Dentists often give the same reasons not to systematize — usually related to time and money. For instance, they might say they don't have time to create formal processes, they don't have time to train employees on them, or they don't want to spend the money to develop and implement processes that cost too much. Days are too busy, and employees and budgets are already stretched to their limits.

But dentists are often surprised to learn that in addition to ensuring patient safety and compliance, systems can also improve efficiency, saving practices both money and time.

FINANCIAL BENEFITS

One of the most common barriers to systematization is the perceived cost. Whether it's the cost of time, tools, or training, many practices are hesitant to invest in these solutions.

But in reality, there are several ways that systems can improve a practice's bottom line:

- **A happy staff stays longer**. Burnout is a big factor in employee turnover, and turnover costs money. Investing in systems that make work easier reduces burnout and boosts retention.
- **Time savings equals money savings**. If a new system saves thirty minutes each day, that translates to two-and-half hours per week or 130 hours a year. Imagine what your team could achieve with that time — or how much you could save in payroll.
- **Emergencies can be avoided**. By proactively addressing inefficiencies and incorporating systems, you can reduce the risk of costly mistakes or unplanned absences due to injury or burnout.
- **Creating systems is an investment, not an expense**. The returns on systems come in time, money, and a stronger, happier team.

> *Creating systems isn't an expense; it's an investment. The returns come in time, money, and a stronger, happier team.*

THE HIDDEN COSTS OF TURNOVER AND BURNOUT

Employee turnover is one of a dental practice's most significant hidden costs. The impact of turnover and onboarding new hires includes lost time (and money), reduced team morale, risks to patient and employee safety, and drained emotional energy. Turnover can also lead to burnout, a growing issue in dental practices driven by heavy workloads and unclear responsibilities.

The good news? Burnout can be managed with the right strategies — and systematization is at the heart of them. Clearly assigned responsibilities and standardized processes reduce stress and help team members feel more in control of their workload. For example, efficient scheduling ensures no one is overburdened, while well-documented procedures empower employees to perform their tasks confidently.

Turnover can also be mitigated by implementing effective systems. Employees who feel valued and supported are more likely to stay. And when life happens, and someone does leave, documented onboarding systems ensure new hires can be trained quickly and efficiently without adding strain to the team.

Systematization isn't just a tool — it's a safety net. By creating and maintaining clear processes, you build a foundation for your team's well-being, ensuring consistency and reducing the inefficiencies that contribute to burnout and turnover.

Many practices have not thought about this, but consider these often-overlooked costs:

Time and Emotional Energy

- *Scrambling to Find a Replacement:* When an employee quits, you're suddenly left with a gap in your team. This requires immediate attention and resources, which distracts you from patient care.
- *Interviewing Candidates:* The time you spend interviewing and vetting candidates not only eats into your schedule but also drains your energy as you attempt to find the right fit while juggling daily operations.

Money and Lost Productivity

- *Reduced Patient Volume:* During the recruitment and onboarding process, you won't be operating with a full team. This means you won't see as many patients as possible, and fewer appointments directly impact your bottom line.
- *Recruitment Costs:* Whether you hire a recruiter or pay for multiple job listing services and platforms (which typically include fees), the cost of finding new talent quickly adds up.

Safety Risks and Team Morale

- **Increased Workload for Remaining Staff:** *When you're down a team member, your remaining employees are stretched thin, which can lead to rushed procedures and overlooked safety protocols. This situation compromises patient care and can lead to mistakes that put the safety of both patients and staff at risk.*
- **Emotional Toll on Your Team:** *The added pressure of covering for a missing employee increases stress, resentment, and burnout among your staff, potentially causing even more turnover.*

Training and Onboarding Time

- **Time-Intensive Training:** *Existing staff must take time away from their own responsibilities to train new hires on critical aspects like safety protocols, infection control, and daily operations. This disrupts regular workflow.*
- **Errors and Learning Curve:** *New hires require time to learn the systems and can make mistakes that cost even more time and money to correct. This adds to the strain on your team and can lead to compliance issues, legacy errors, and potential injuries — all of which create further setbacks.*

Impact on Focus and Mission

- **Loss of Focus:** *All these disruptions distract your attention and your team's focus from the core mission of your practice: serving and caring for patients. The more time you spend fixing the problems caused by turnover, the less energy you have to invest in patient care and practice growth.*

Investing in a well-structured system and cultivating a stable team minimizes these hidden costs, saving your practice valuable time and money. Systems also help create a strong foundation for growth, ensuring your practice thrives.

DR. STOUT'S APPROACH TO ENDING OVERTIME

Dr. Stout watched the clock tick past 5:15 p.m. For months, his team had been clocking out late — sometimes as much as an hour after their last patient left. He frowned as he considered the added labor costs of this extra time.

"Why does it take everyone an extra half hour or hour to leave each day?" Dr. Stout asked Tina, his office manager. "The overtime cost is starting to get out of hand. They should be able to complete everything by 4:30, but they're not getting out of here until 5:15 or 5:30." He estimated that these inefficiencies were adding hundreds of dollars to each month's payroll. This needed to be fixed, and soon.

Tina, caught off guard, replied, "I don't know. I hadn't thought about it."

"Tomorrow, I'm going to watch what they do after the last patient leaves to try to figure out what's happening," Dr. Stout said, determined to get to the bottom of this.

The next evening, he quietly watched. At first, the lively activity looked productive, but as he continued observing, inefficiencies became glaringly obvious. Hygienists scrambled to finish their chart notes after cleaning operatories. An assistant wiped down counters, only for another employee to repeat the same task minutes later. Supplies were counted and restocked redundantly.

The realization hit him: It wasn't that his team was unproductive — they just didn't have clear expectations. They were duplicating efforts and wasting time, which stretched the workday unnecessarily.

The next morning, Dr. Stout met with Tina to address the issue. "We need a plan for who does what in the evenings," he said firmly. "They are duplicating their efforts and wasting time."

Tina nodded, "Okay, let's list everything we need to do before closing."

"Yeah, that's a good place to start," he responded. "Then let's make a checklist with all the tasks and who is responsible for each one so everyone knows what to do."

By the end of the week, Tina and Dr. Stout had outlined all the evening tasks and assigned them to team members based on skill level and roles. At the following week's morning huddle, they introduced the new task system.

Tina held up the printed checklist she had laminated for easy reuse, explaining, "This is our new evening routine. We've divided up the end-of-day tasks, and everyone has specific jobs to do."

Laura, a hygienist, sighed in relief. "Oh, I'm really glad you did this," she admitted. "I've always been unsure about exactly what I was supposed to do."

Tammy, a dental assistant, raised her hand, "Could we do this for the mornings, too?"

Dr. Stout smiled, pleased with the feedback. "We'll do that next," he replied.

Within days, the impact was obvious. Hygienists now knew to finish their chart notes first while the dental assistants focused on cleaning the rooms. The sterile tech finished instrument processing and cleaning up the sterilization area. The new system flowed seamlessly, with every team member working in sync.

If you've ever felt overwhelmed by inefficiencies in your practice, Dr. Stout's story shows how a simple checklist can transform your workflow. The key is to start small and prioritize clarity for tasks and responsibilities.

The biggest change wasn't just having a checklist; it was the team's approach to managing tasks and time. A single, standardized system eliminated uncertainty, stress, and inefficiencies.

"I DON'T HAVE TIME" IS COSTING YOU MORE THAN YOU THINK

Burnout among dental professionals is at an all-time high. According to the American Dental Association, 13 percent of dentists have experienced depression, and 16 percent have faced anxiety — a big increase from previous years. New dentists are particularly vulnerable due to student loan burdens, income pressures, and the challenges of building a practice. Since the pandemic, general practitioners report feeling overworked or struggling to balance their workload, with 37 percent saying they're "too busy to treat all patients requesting appointments."[4]

With so much pressure, it's tempting to think, "I don't have time to create these systems." The truth is you can't afford NOT to. Every hour you spend now developing systems will save dozens of hours and reduce stress over the long term. **This is an investment in your future.**

Dr. Stout's team is a good example of the benefits of taking time to implement systems. The simple act of creating an end-of-day checklist saved his practice hundreds of dollars each month and reduced team burnout. Staff went home on time, confident and happy, instead of frazzled and overworked.

Get Help When You Need It

If the idea of creating all these systems feels overwhelming, consider consulting with compliance experts. Reputable companies can provide detailed SOP templates and assist with creating systems tailored to your practice.

As you experience the benefits of systematization — time saved, reduced stress, and increased staff confidence — you'll see how transformative it is. **Start small, build momentum, and watch your practice thrive.**

---

4   American Dental Association, "Burnout among Dental Professionals," accessed November 20, 2024, https://adanews.ada.org/new-dentist/2022/may/the-burden-of-burnout/.

TAKE ACTION: MAKE YOUR END-OF-DAY CHECKLIST

Are you ready to streamline your end-of-day process like Dr. Stout did? A customized checklist tailored to your practice's needs is key to your team's efficiency. Use the steps below and the sample chart on the next page to get started.

Follow these steps to create your checklist:

1. **List all tasks:** Write down every task that must be completed before your team leaves for the day.

END-OF-DAY TASKS	PERSON RESPONSIBLE

2. **Assign responsibilities:** Match each task to the team member or job title best suited for it based on their role.

3. **Create your checklist:** Organize the tasks in a clear, easy-to-follow list. Ask employees to check off their tasks at the end of each day.

Want a pre-made template? Visit GoodDentistBook.com to download your free End-of-Day Checklist and jumpstart your systematization efforts. A sample hard copy template is also provided at the end of this chapter.

END-OF-DAY DUTIES

DUTY	THE PERSON OR JOB TITLE RESPONSIBLE	MON DATE	TUES DATE	WED DATE	THURS DATE	FRI DATE
Complete chart notes						
Clean patient rooms/operatories						
Empty water bottles						
Finish sterilization by running the remaining instruments and putting any clean instruments away						
Check sterilization logs						
Empty and clean the ultrasonic cleaner						
Evacuation system cleaned for water lines						
Turn off: compressors, N_2O, O_2, Ultrasonic, handpiece oilers, purifiers, and TVs						
Log off computers and turn off monitors						
Restock supplies throughout the clinic						
Clean and declutter the lab						
Clean and declutter the sterilization area						
Sweep operatories, sterilization, and lab areas						
Take trash out of operatories, sterilization, front office, and bathrooms						
Turn off lights						

CHAPTER 8

HARNESSING THE POWER OF MOMENTUM

Success is the sum of small efforts, repeated day in and day out.
— ROBERT COLLIER

Experience has shown us that all dental practices have similar procedural bottlenecks. There are specific moments during the day when things can go smoothly or awry. Effective systems can help you navigate these transitions and create positive momentum in your practice. It's important to focus on small, intentional changes to accomplish this. Collectively, these small changes will help create positive momentum by providing small wins that add up to big results.

As you develop your systems, expect some hiccups along the way. Rely on the SAFER framework to help you continually adapt and change processes so you can create a system tailored specifically to your practice's needs. By addressing issues and fine-tuning systems, you'll improve outcomes and empower your team to work for positive change, resulting in long-term success for your practice.

BUILD MOMENTUM THROUGH SYSTEMS

Momentum isn't created by fixing one problem. It's built by stacking small improvements over time. Each improvement can inspire your team to identify more opportunities for growth. This is the power of momentum: Small wins fuel confidence and drive further progress.

As you develop processes, know that you are not alone in the challenges you face. Many dental practices experience very similar issues, and addressing these common bottlenecks can make all the difference, as you'll see in the following situation at Sunrise Dental Group.

The Case of the Missing Instrument

On a busy Monday morning at Sunrise Dental Group, Danny was rushing around the office, sweat dripping down his forehead. How did he miss the condenser? He thought he had put it on the tray, but keeping track of which instruments the doctor needed for each procedure was overwhelming.

Panicked, Danny hurried into the sterilization area, his mind racing. He scanned the clean cassettes on the shelves, knowing that if he opened one, all the instruments would need to be repackaged and re-sterilized — something the office didn't have time for. With the patient already waiting in the chair, Danny felt he had no choice. He opened a clean package, retrieved the condenser, and placed the remaining instruments on the dirty side.

Rushing back to the room, he handed the condenser to Dr. Kim. "Here it is," Danny said, his voice shaky.

Dr. Kim responded sharply, "Thank you. Let's not let that happen again."

Danny nodded, trying to refocus on the procedure while feeling anxious and upset.

Meanwhile, Katie, another dental assistant, went into the sterilization area to prepare her tray for the next patient. She immediately noticed a problem: Her clean cassette was missing from the cabinet. Then she saw it — the opened package sitting on the dirty side. With only five minutes until her next patient arrived, Katie scrambled to retrieve a cassette from the autoclave. She put the cassette on her tray and reached for new sterilization packaging to reprocess the cassette Danny had left, knowing it would be needed later. However, she quickly realized they had run out of sterilizer wrapping paper, leaving her unable to complete the task.

The domino effect was in full swing. One oversight had spiraled into cascading delays, mounting stress, and disrupted workflows for the entire team.

Later that day, Dr. Kim pulled the office manager aside to discuss the issue. "Danny didn't have the condenser on the tray today. Mrs. Smith and I had to wait while he found it. Why does this keep happening?"

The office manager frowned, considering his question. "I'll look into it," she replied. "It seems like a bigger problem with managing instruments and workflows."

Recognizing the growing strain on the team, the office manager called us in to assess their systems. As we observed, it became clear that the staff's dedication wasn't the issue — it was the lack of clear, efficient processes. Hard work alone wasn't enough to prevent recurring mistakes that cost time, energy, and confidence.

Common Bottlenecks

At Sunrise Dental Group, the root causes were plain to see: unclear instrument setups and a single autoclave that couldn't keep up with demand. These bottlenecks led to unnecessary delays, increased team stress, and compromised workflows.

These challenges aren't unique. Many dental practices experience similar issues, which often fall into a few key categories:

Sterilization Delays: These can be addressed by adding more instruments or equipment (such as a second autoclave) to handle patient volume efficiently.

Scheduling Challenges: Automated scheduling systems can help manage cancellations, balance workloads, and reduce downtime.

Supply Restocking: Assigning specific team members to handle inventory and scheduling regular supply checks ensures materials are always available when needed.

By identifying these common bottlenecks and devising systems to resolve them, practices can achieve more than just immediate relief. These changes pave the way for smoother operations, less stress, and a stronger foundation for future growth.

At Sunrise Dental Group, adding a second autoclave addressed the immediate sterilization bottleneck. But the team didn't stop there. They also did the following:

- *Streamlined morning and evening routines to ensure everyone knew their responsibilities.*
- *Developed a tray setup system with laminated photos to reduce confusion.*
- *Implemented a continuous restocking process to prevent supply shortages.*

Periodically reassessing systems and protocols is essential to keep a practice operating efficiently. Reevaluating processes and improving or adding to them can help minimize the likelihood of bottlenecks that cost you time, money, and energy. Sometimes, it's helpful to have an outside company observe workflows and systems to help objectively identify areas for improvement.

Continuous Improvement

- **10-Minute Tidy**: Set aside 10 minutes at the end of each week for small improvements, like reorganizing a storage area or reviewing a checklist.
- **Pilot New Ideas**: Test new workflow changes on a small scale before rolling them out practice-wide. This minimizes risk and allows for revisions and adjustments.
- **Rotating "Fix It" Weeks**: Rotate focus among team members or areas of the practice (e.g., sterilization, patient scheduling) to spotlight and resolve inefficiencies.
- **Team-Led Training**: Let team members lead short lessons on their areas of expertise or systems they've improved, encouraging ownership and peer learning.
- **Storytelling for Success**: Share quick stories at meetings about how systems solved problems to inspire ongoing commitment to momentum-building efforts.

ENGAGE YOUR TEAM FOR LASTING CHANGE

When team members are involved in creating solutions, they feel empowered and take ownership of the process. At Sunrise, the team worked together to identify bottlenecks, test solutions, and refine existing systems. This collaboration didn't just improve workflows — it strengthened the team's morale and commitment to excellence.

There are a number of ways you can involve your team:

- Hold a brainstorming session to identify recurring issues.
- Assign roles based on strengths to ensure responsibilities are manageable.
- Celebrate small wins, such as completing a new SOP or improving patient flow.

When everyone contributes to the process, the practice becomes a place of shared accountability and pride.

ONE STEP AT A TIME

Momentum isn't built overnight, but every small improvement adds up to significant progress. By addressing bottlenecks, empowering your team, and refining systems, you create a practice that runs more smoothly, reduces stress, and delivers better patient care.

The key is to start where you are, take one step at a time, and celebrate each success along the way.

As you move forward, remember that sustainable growth comes not from perfection but from consistent effort. Momentum builds when you commit to continuous improvement, inspiring your team and strengthening your practice with every change.

Small steps each day lead to big results over time.
— UNKNOWN

Momentum is the driving force behind lasting success and the key to building it lies in your systems. Each small step — creating a script, refining a workflow, or assigning roles more effectively — leads to larger improvements. These adjustments reduce stress, strengthen teamwork, and improve patient outcomes. Try the following to help build momentum in your practice:

1. Observe your practice.

Spend thirty minutes just watching. Observe how tasks flow in your practice. Focus on areas where processes slow down, mistakes occur, or frustration builds. Write down your observations, and identify one area where a system could make a difference.

Some things to consider while observing:

- *Are roles and responsibilities clearly defined?*
- *Are repetitive tasks taking longer than they should?*
- *Are there moments when the team seems stressed or unsure of what to do next?*

2. Reflect and brainstorm with your team.

Once you've identified a bottleneck, brainstorm with your team. Consider simple solutions that would improve the process. Refer back to chapter 5 where we discussed SOPs. There, you'll find suggestions on how to document new systems.

3. Periodically review systems

Periodically, take a moment with your team to review and revisit processes. Find out if things are still working and revise or add to them if needed.

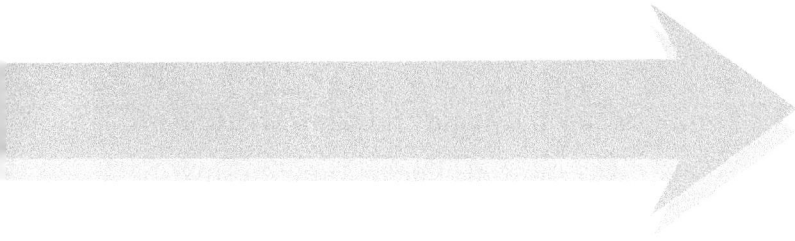

CHAPTER 9

MAKE YOUR NEXT MOVE

In the end, we only regret the chances we didn't take.
— **LEWIS CARROLL**

Running a dental practice is about so much more than safety and compliance. It's about creating an environment where your team thrives, your patients feel cared for, and your goals as a business owner come to life. Compliance systems aren't just about meeting regulations — they're the bridge to the vision you had when you first began your journey.

RECLAIM YOUR PASSION

Think back to when you decided to embark on this career. You likely dreamed of making a difference in people's lives, improving their health, and building a practice you could be proud of. Compliance and systems may not have been part of that dream, but they are the tools that can make it possible. They free you from the constant stress of putting out fires and allow you to focus on the work you're truly passionate about.

One client perfectly captured this feeling when they said: "Having written and well-organized documents and systems gives me confidence knowing my employees and company are protected. Now, I can focus on my patients, knowing everything else is handled."

Implementing compliance systems helps you meet regulations and achieve peace of mind. Imagine walking into your practice and being able to focus solely on patient care because everything else is handled. Your team knows exactly what to do, patients are satisfied, and you have the freedom to prioritize growth and improvement.

REFLECT, REALIGN, AND REIGNITE

Take a moment to reflect on your practice and your vision. Understanding the connection between systems and your vision can open up countless possibilities, including the opportunity to rediscover your purpose and regain control over your time and energy.

Personal Goals

Reflect on these prompts to help identify your ultimate goals and areas for improvement. Write down your thoughts below:

1. **What would you like more of?**
   - *Time and connections with patients*
   - *Team collaboration and synergy*
   - *Consistent, predictable routines that reduce stress*
   - *Higher employee morale and lower turnover*

_____

_____

_____
_____
_____
_____
_____
_____

2. **What would you like less of?**
   ○ *Turnover — time lost being short-staffed and training new hires*
   ○ *Compliance worries — fears of inspections and violations*
   ○ *Emergencies — problems that are preventable*
   ○ *Disorganization — leading to wasted time and inefficiencies*

_____
_____
_____
_____
_____
_____
_____

3. **Now, ask yourself two things:**
   ○ **If you could achieve some (or all!) of these changes, how would you feel?**
     » Proud? Relieved? Fulfilled?
   ○ **What would these changes allow you to do?**
     » Spend more time with your family? Grow your practice? Deliver better patient care?

Reflection and Planning Tools

- **Vision Mapping:** Create a visual map of where you see your practice in one, five, and ten years. Use this as a guide to prioritize system improvements.
- **Quarterly Reflection Sessions:** Schedule time to reflect on what's working and identify areas where you can align systems with your long-term goals.
- **Team Vision Workshop:** Collaborate with your team to craft a shared vision for the practice. Discuss how systems can help achieve this vision.
- **Empowerment Stories:** Share success stories (like Dr. Lisa or Dr. Sanchez) with your team to inspire them to embrace systematization.

Purpose

Now it's time to reconnect with the reason you started your practice. Reflect on goals, worries, and initial motivations. This is the first step toward taking control and building the practice you really want. **Systems are your tools, but your vision is the blueprint.**

Use the prompts below to reflect on your "why" to help you identify practical ways you can align systems to match your purpose and create more time for what truly matters.

1. **Why did you become a dentist?**
   - What were your personal and professional motivations for choosing this career and starting your practice?

_____

_____

_____

_____

2. **How could a system help you focus more on your purpose?**

   ○ Think about a recurring task or bottleneck in your practice. How could improving this system give you more time to focus on your "why"?

_____

_____

_____

_____

Systems are your tools, but your vision is the blueprint.

Taking Action, One Step at a Time

- **"One System at a Time" Initiative:** Focus on improving one system per month. Start with the most pressing bottleneck and build momentum gradually.
- **First Step Exercise:** Ask yourself, "What's one small change I can make today that will have a positive ripple effect?" Act on it immediately.
- **Professional Sabbaticals**: Block time for yourself to step away from daily operations and brainstorm ways to align your practice with your bigger goals.
- **Mentorship Opportunities**: Use your streamlined practice as a model to mentor younger dentists or inspire peers in the industry.

ONE DENTIST'S BREAKTHROUGH

For many dentists, rediscovering their purpose means regaining control over their time and energy. Dr. Lisa's story is a good example of what's possible when systems align with your vision.

Dr. Lisa had always dreamed of a European vacation with her family but felt trapped by the day-to-day challenges of running her practice. Daily tasks, staff turnover, and compliance worries consumed her time.

After implementing the SAFER Compliance System, everything changed. Within a year, the practice was running so smoothly that Lisa realized she could step away without fear of the wheels falling off. Confident that her team could handle operations in her absence, she booked that long-awaited European vacation.

She explored Paris, Rome, and Barcelona with her family for two glorious weeks, knowing her practice was flourishing back home. "I never thought I'd be able to take this trip," she told us. "The systems we created gave me back my life."

Dr. Lisa's journey shows that it's possible to regain control, prioritize what matters, and build the life you've always wanted.

RETURN ON INVESTMENT: YOUR TIME AND SANITY

While compliance may feel like a burden at times, it's actually a powerful ally in your pursuit of excellence. Even if the only thing compliance systems did was reduce turnover, wouldn't that be worth it?

Of course, it's NOT the only thing compliance systems can do. They also protect your patients, safeguard your practice, and ensure your business stands the test of time.

By embracing systems and processes, you're not only avoiding risks but also actively investing in your team, your patients, and your peace of mind. The systems you build today will pay off tenfold in creating a thriving, well-respected practice that operates with precision and care.

Your time and peace of mind are invaluable. Partnering with experts to handle compliance efficiently is an investment in your practice and your life.

Even if the only thing compliance systems did was reduce turnover, wouldn't that be worth it?

IF DR. CASSIE SANCHEZ CAN DO IT, SO CAN YOU

Dr. Cassie Sanchez was a meticulously diligent dental student, and unlike many of her peers, she was already thinking about running her own practice. As she quietly took copious notes in class, Cassie was planning her strategy. Her classmates saw her as reserved, but Cassie was preparing for what came next and already planning for the practice she wanted.

In her first job with Dr. Thomas Everett, who believed in systematizing everything, Cassie learned the power of clear processes. He documented everything in the office: tray setups, dental procedures, and sterilization workflows. This preparation gave her a head start when she opened her own practice, where she quickly implemented systems for onboarding, patient care, and even scheduling Fridays off.

As her practice grew, Cassie automated reminders and follow-ups to lighten her team's workload and improve patient care. Within a year, her systems were running so smoothly that she managed her practice in a standard nine-to-five schedule.

At a dental society luncheon, her classmates expressed their struggles with long hours and burnout. Cassie shared her approach to systematization and how it allowed her to see ten patients a day while maintaining a work-life balance. Her peers were stunned.

Dr. Sanchez's journey shows how consistent systems and deliberate action can create a thriving practice.

CREATE THE FUTURE YOU WANT

The best way to predict your future is to create it. Dream big, but start small. You have what it takes. Each improvement you make builds a foundation for success, whether it's automating reminders, refining protocols, or creating on-boarding processes for new team members.

> *Dream big, start small, and take control of your practice.*

You are not simply a great dentist; you are an entrepreneur! You want more for your patients, your staff, and yourself. Every SOP you create and implement strengthens the foundation of your practice and sets a standard of excellence. When systems are in place, you can take a step back, focus on growth, or take a vacation and know your team is aligned with your vision.

But this work isn't just about you. By prioritizing systems, you're creating something bigger than yourself. You're building a legacy of safety, trust, and excellence that benefits your team, patients, and community. Your efforts inspire others in the industry and demonstrate what's possible with the right tools and mindset.

When your practice runs smoothly, everyone wins. Your team feels pride in their work. Your patients notice the exceptional care, and your reputation as a leader grows.

It all starts with one step: building the systems that will carry your practice into the future.

You don't need anyone's permission to take that step — you already have the knowledge, authority, and vision to transform your practice. What's left is action.

> *You don't have to be great to start, but you have to start to be great.*
> — ZIG ZIGLAR

CONGRATULATIONS!

You've reached the end of this book, a significant step in your journey toward greatness for your practice, your team, and yourself. By now, you understand the power of systems to drive safety, efficiency, and freedom in your practice.

Start small, stay consistent, and let each improvement build on the last. Your practice's success depends on the actions you take today.

The tools are in your hands — take the first step now. Your team will thrive, your patients will feel the difference, and your future self will thank you for making this commitment to excellence.

Let's move forward together!

The best way to predict the future is to create it.

TAKE ACTION: CREATE YOUR GAME PLAN

You now have all the tools you need to get started. Remember: Small actions can have a big impact. Each step builds momentum, creating a practice that's safer, more efficient, and poised for growth. Think about the SAFER process and choose a place to begin.

1. Review the SAFER Compliance System steps:

Survey: Assess your current systems and identify gaps.

Architect: Design clear, step-by-step protocols tailored to your practice.

Facilitate: Delegate responsibilities and automate repetitive tasks.

Educate: Train your team and keep them updated on compliance standards.

Review: Regularly refine your systems to stay effective and aligned with your goals.

2. Select one step to focus on this month. For example:

- Conduct a survey to identify compliance gaps in your practice.
- Create a written protocol for one key process.
- Schedule a team training to ensure everyone is aligned.
- Set a specific, measurable goal for that step and commit to achieving it by the end of the month.

Take the Next Step with Support

Many practice owners find that professional guidance simplifies compliance and provides invaluable peace of mind. As one client shared, "Having written and well-organized documents and systems gives me confidence knowing my employees and company are protected."

This confidence lets you focus on your passion for patient care while knowing your practice is secure and compliant.

You don't have to do this alone.

Schedule a consultation today at GoodDentistBook.com, and together, we'll create a customized plan for your practice. Your team, your patients, and your future will thank you.

ACKNOWLEDGEMENTS

To Frank Plaisted, my SCORE mentor — thank you for introducing me to the "franchise model" and providing me with the foundation for scaling my business.

To Pastor Jim Baker (Wealth with God) and Pedro Adeo (100X) — your mentorship has transformed my understanding of divine inheritance and empowered me to walk boldly in my purpose.

To Ed Rush, my business coach and source of endless inspiration — your encouragement to write this book and your constant push to dream bigger have been invaluable.

ABOUT KELLI

KELLI NGARIKI is a passionate compliance consultant, business owner, and advocate for streamlined systems in dental practices. As the owner of Healthcare Compliance Associates, she has dedicated her career to helping dental professionals improve their practices through efficient systems and simplified compliance processes that meet OSHA, HIPAA, and infection control standards. Her proven SAFER Compliance System empowers practices to enhance efficiency, elevate patient care, and build stronger, happier teams.

With master's degrees in organizational management and education, Kelli combines her academic expertise with practical experience to deliver actionable solutions that truly make a difference. She is surprisingly good at two things: developing and streamlining systems and making difficult topics easy to understand. This unique ability has earned her glowing reviews from clients, many of whom describe her training as fun, engaging, and transformative.

One of her favorite memories is speaking at an Oregon Dental Association event, where a long-time dentist praised her session as *"the best infection control training he had ever taken — and he had taken many."* Kelli's ideal clients are dentists who strive to improve their practices for the benefit of their patients, employees, and themselves.

Her approachable teaching style and commitment to excellence have made her a sought-after speaker and trusted partner for dental practices across Oregon and beyond.

When she's not helping practices thrive, Kelli lives in Springfield, Oregon, with her husband and two sons. As a proud mom to boys with Fragile X syndrome, Kelli deeply values systems and routines that create balance and reduce stress both at work and at home.

CONTACT INFO

Website: GoodDentistBook.com
Email: Kelli@OshaHipaaTraining.com
LinkedIn: Kelli-Ngariki
Facebook: OshaHipaaTraining
Instagram: @HealthcareComplianceAssoc

BE AN
EXCELLENT
DENTIST
AND TRANSFORM YOUR PRACTICE

Compliance doesn't have to be complicated. The experts at Healthcare Compliance Associates will help you implement proven safety, efficiency, and growth strategies. Together, we'll create systems that reduce stress, enhance patient care, and empower your team to thrive.

Achieve more than compliance—achieve excellence.

THE RESULTS YOU CAN EXPECT:

- More time and less stress.
- A safer, fully compliant practice.
- A confident, empowered team with clear, actionable systems.

READY TO GET STARTED?

1. Visit: GoodDentistBook.com or scan the QR code
2. Schedule your free 25-minute compliance strategy call.
   - Uncover strengths and gaps in your compliance systems.
   - Pinpoint areas to boost safety and efficiency.
   - Get clear, actionable strategies to simplify your practice.
3. Relax – we'll handle the rest!

Let's simplify compliance and systems to create a practice that functions seamlessly, achieves excellence, and reflects your commitment to greatness.

Visit GoodDentistBook.com today to schedule your free call!

LOOKING FOR A
DYNAMIC
SPEAKER
FOR YOUR NEXT EVENT?

Looking for a dynamic speaker who makes compliance and safety simple, practical, and fun? Kelli Ngariki, MAOM, MAEd, CEO of Healthcare Compliance Associates, simplifies compliance and safety for dental professionals with engaging, interactive sessions that inspire and equip audiences with actionable strategies.

WHY CHOOSE KELLI?

- **Engaging & Memorable:** Humor and real-world examples make compliance practical and fun.
- **Tailored Content:** Sessions on infection control, OSHA, HIPAA, and more, designed for dental professionals.
- **Proven Expertise:** A blend of academic knowledge and hands-on experience for maximum impact.

POPULAR TOPICS

- How Systems Transform Your Practice from Average to Excellent
- Infection Control
- OSHA & HIPAA Essentials
- Cultural Competency

MAKE YOUR NEXT EVENT UNFORGETTABLE!

Book Kelli Ngariki today for your dental conference or meeting.

Scan the QR code to book a meeting or call 541-345-3875 ext. 1.
www.linkedin.com/in/kelli-ngariki-46800820